*On Religious Life:
William James and I*

On Religious Life: William James and I

An Affectionate Rumination

Cordell Strug

WIPF & STOCK · Eugene, Oregon

ON RELIGIOUS LIFE: WILLIAM JAMES AND I
An Affectionate Rumination

Copyright © 2016 Cordell Strug. All rights reserved. Except for brief quotations in critical publications or reviews, no part of this book may be reproduced in any manner without prior written permission from the publisher. Write: Permissions, Wipf and Stock Publishers, 199 W. 8th Ave., Suite 3, Eugene, OR 97401.

Wipf & Stock
An Imprint of Wipf and Stock Publishers
199 W. 8th Ave., Suite 3
Eugene, OR 97401

www.wipfandstock.com

PAPERBACK ISBN: 978-1-4982-9031-9
HARDCOVER ISBN: 978-1-4982-9033-3
EBOOK ISBN: 978-1-4982-9032-6

Manufactured in the U.S.A.   JUNE 14, 2016

To all those who have found companions in the people of the past *ruminari*, Latin, "chew over again"

He swore by all possible deities.
—STEPHEN CRANE, DESCRIBING AN OFFICER'S PROFANITY,
THE RED BADGE OF COURAGE

Contents

Preface | ix

Acknowledgments | xi

Part One: Finding a Companion in the Past | 1

Part Two: Evil, Evolution, and the Creativity of Chaos: William James and the Human Plight | 13

Part Three: William James and the Gods (Revisited): A(nother) Peek at the Conceptual Underbelly of *The Varieties of Religious Experience*
- 1. *Introductions(s), Then and Now* | 26
- 2. *The Use and Abuse of Psychology* | 30
- 3. *The Meaning of God in Human Experience* | 45
- 4. *Tradition and the Individual Believer* | 59
- 5. *Saints in the Hands of an Empirical Philosopher* | 80
- 6. *Search for a Spiritual Landscape* | 106

Part Four: Ave atque Vale | 131

Bibliography | 141

Preface

This book is the record of one religious person's lifelong engagement with one great philosopher's religious vision. I came to William James as a student, with scholarly interests and dreams of an academic life. I also came as someone with a strong religious background, looking for a different, more expansive way to be religious. Both James and the fortunes of life ended up surprising me.

I have spent my life as a Lutheran pastor, not as a scholar, and William James has accompanied me, not as a subject for study but as a living presence. Now, at my life's closing, I want to look back and chew over again what attracted me to James, what I found in his vision, what changed me as I wrestled with his work, and what he has meant in my life. It was his great set of lectures on *The Varieties of Religious Experience* that challenged and changed me the most, so the heart of this book is a revisiting of the themes of that work, weighing them after a religious life that took a different path than the one James offered, through a different and, in some ways, a harsher world than he might have imagined.

Acknowledgments

SEVERAL PEOPLE DESERVE THANKS for agreeing to look at this writing as it was taking shape and, thus, making me feel less alone: Bill Edminster, Peter Geisendorfer-Lindgren, Gary and Ruth Halverson, Arland Jacobson, Joyce Matuszewich, Mary Preus, and Gary Taylor. Paul Sponheim and Paulette Leonard provided thoughtful commentary. Mary Carol Strug provided receptive listening and timely advice.

Many people of long ago deserve thanks for leading me to William James and forcing me to think deeply about his work: J. Weldon Smith III, Richard Grabau, William Rowe, Calvin Schrag, and the students in my Philosophy of Religion classes.

I must thank as well the gracious and efficient people at Wipf and Stock Publishers, who make a daunting process seem surmountable.

Finally, I am once again indebted to my partner in literary adventures, Sylvia Ruud, the initiating force and guiding spirit of this work; without her, it would still be nothing but random notes and idle dreams.

Part One

Finding a Companion in the Past

I ATTENDED A TINY liberal arts college in Jacksonville, Illinois, a town that once called itself "the Athens of the Midwest." It was a boast I was happy to share. MacMurray College had the redbrick buildings, the sprawling fields, and the tree-lined cobblestone streets of a typically picturesque small college. The library and the chapel faced each other, like two contenders for the human spirit, across an open field where the women played field hockey. (MacMurray had been founded as a women's college before the Civil War and had only recently begun admitting men. There was a beloved story that Ann Rutledge, Lincoln's first love, had been a student.) There was another college in Jacksonville, Illinois College, which William Jennings Bryan had attended, as well as schools for the blind and the deaf. It was a pretty serious community of learning and public service, though I should probably mention that the town also made Ferris wheels.

The year I came to MacMurray, the single most well known quotation on campus was from a *Time* magazine story on the folk singer Judy Collins: she said she had spent "one mummifying year" as a student there. It was true that the sixties had not quite reached MacMurray, though they soon would. We had a dress code, women were locked in the dormitories after 10:30, chapel was mandatory (complete with sign-in sheets), and no cars were allowed on campus. Out-of-state students who drove themselves to Jacksonville had to turn in their keys to their housemaster. (When I drive past our local high school and see the cars of the teen-aged students who drive themselves daily, I shake my head in wonder.) Students from . . . well, almost anywhere else in America thought they had blundered through a time warp and fallen into the nineteenth century. But since I had gone to high school in the thirteenth century, an all-male boarding school in a Benedictine monastery, I thought MacMurray was a most wonderful and exciting place.

It was in this lovely physical setting that I began to explore seriously that greater spiritual palace of cultural memory. It was there I met and grew to know the philosopher who would be one of my lifelong companions, William James. I met him the way we meet many of the people important to us, through the words of others.

I love the magic of learning, how it fills in and fills out the world around us, by stories and by names, by marking paths and by warning of dead ends. I love how it expands communities, summoning up the ghosts of the past and bidding them to come abide with us. This begins from the day we open our eyes and wonder where our next meal is coming from. That is, our gift of cultural memory is more fundamental than the gifts of cultural instruments.

But, with the invention of writing, once we ourselves read and write, the power of expanding life is literally in our own hands. Access to a good library might give us the illusion that we can do without the elders and the bards of earlier times, those who told the stories and sang the songs of the past, who brought it to life and marked out what was worthy in it. With computers and the internet, this has become a full-blown delusion. Its dangers are writ large in what passes for public debate among us.

But one of the central things I took from studying James's pragmatism was how vitally important our particular intellectual heritage is, a heritage of both persons and ideas; how much it shapes the pursuit of knowledge. Though James might be taken as a philosopher of the new, it's hard to overestimate the weight of the past in his vision of learning and understanding. I don't mean to reargue the pragmatic theory of truth, but I think, in general, the dimension of time in James's notion of truth, as well as in his sense of how knowledge works, is unappreciated, when it's not distorted by shallow criticism. Just how our ideas get us to what we want to know is an essential part of what we know.

In any case, it seemed to me only fitting, since this is a book on William James, to tell a little of my elders, the particular people that pointed me toward James, and the particular steps I took to get to him. In my church, we have a number of ceremonies where the hands of the old are laid on the heads of the young; it's a symbolic act that only dramatizes a common and indispensable human act: the transmission of what we love from the community of the past to the community of the future, a transmission that creates communion.

The head of the Philosophy and Religion Department at MacMurray had the wonderful name of J. Weldon Smith III. He was an athletic man with dark, striking looks. Someone told me he had played third base for the Yale baseball team. He chain-smoked Camel cigarettes and his seminars were conducted in thick clouds of smoke. He drove a black British sportscar and had very much the manner of a squire come among the rustics to enlighten them. I still occasionally wear the tweed sports coat, now threadbare, that I bought as a senior so I could look like him.

I had originally thought I would major in English; in fact, the courses I continued to love the most were my literature courses. But after I had taken Dr. Smith's Introduction to Philosophy, I realized I would be failing myself if I didn't study philosophy: it was both more difficult and somehow more essential to me.

Dr. Smith was an ordained Methodist minister and, like most theologians of the time, was drawn philosophically to the existentialists and phenomenologists. They were a bit more promising as partners in dialogue than Bertrand Russell or Rudolf Carnap. (Wittgenstein turned out, interestingly enough, to be a wild card here.) Writers like Kierkegaard, Nietzsche, Sartre, and Heidegger, even when hostile to religion, at least seemed to offer common ground to fight over.

But Dr. Smith was also a crusader for American studies and wanted students to appreciate American religious thinkers like Jonathan Edwards and Reinhold Niebuhr. One of the spectacular highlights of the mandatory core course in the history of philosophy and religion was his performance of Edwards's sermon "Sinners in the Hands of an Angry God"—which I heard him time perfectly to end just before the class bell.

He revered William James. He never tired of pointing out that, when John Wild gave a course at Harvard on phenomenology, he used for his text James's *Principles of Psychology*. With James, there was the grappling with concrete experience, the breadth of sympathy with all human doing and dreaming, the passion and the vision that we were looking for in the existentialists and phenomenologists, but it came without jargon, in a clear, affable, generous, deceptively simple American voice. It came without arrogance: I can't imagine Sartre or Heidegger describing their philosophies

On Religious Life: William James and I

as "a new name for some old ways of thinking," as James did. It came, too, in lovely prose that was a pleasure to read, something that was probably as important as anything else during my first struggles. It came, finally, with a happy willingness to investigate all our ways of knowing and living, from science to religion, logic to mysticism.

We probably spent, in our various classes and seminars, as much time studying theologians as philosophers, certainly among modern figures: Martin Buber, Dietrich Bonhoeffer, Rudolf Bultmann, Paul Tillich. I wrote my senior thesis on Bultmann and demythologizing. Looking back, I suspect this helped set James off as a purely philosophical figure. Anyway, without being the only or even the most important thinker I worked on, he was, by the time I graduated, set firmly in my gallery of intellectual heroes.

(I acquired, as an undergraduate, another, stranger connection to James. I had been working on the campus newspaper and got the chance to attend a college newspaper conference in Washington, D.C. I think I remember Ben Bradlee being there, as well as Tom Hayden. Somehow I found myself in a small group talking to Walter Lippmann, the venerable journalist and political commentator. Could I have been photographed with him by someone who wanted a shot of Lippmann and "some students"? I'm sure I shook hands with him. Now here's my connection: Lippmann had not only been James's student at Harvard; they had met weekly for tea in James's home. I was thrilled to have so close a link to James himself, though such a link in the mid-twentieth century was probably common among American academic and literary figures. When network theorists began talking about being connected to everyone on the planet by no more than five intermediaries—or six degrees of separation—I had fun extending the theory to the past and counting my degrees to Hemingway [from James through Gertrude Stein] and almost any late nineteenth-century writer [from James through Henry James], but it was James I was delighted to be close to. And I think this way of grasping our human closeness would have pleased him, both as a reminder of how small the human community is in the vast universe and as a sign of the homely strangeness of the world, its irreducible and impenetrable contingency.)

I spent my first year of grad school at Indiana University, where I had a front row seat to watch academic politics purge the Philosophy Department of everything interesting in it. I moved on to Purdue University, where I again found myself comfortably within the nineteenth century and happy to be there.

Finding a Companion in the Past

Graduate students taught some of the undergraduate philosophy courses, and I was assigned to teach—though I'm not sure why—both Introduction to Ethics and Introduction to the Philosophy of Religion. Perhaps I struck everyone as reasonably moral and religious.

We were given, as I look back, a surprising amount of latitude in how we approached and what we required in our courses. The truth, no doubt, was that no one cared that much what we did. I thought of my courses as analogous to first-year language courses, providing a foundation for further work, formal or otherwise. So when I taught Philosophy of Religion, we would do the arguments for the existence of God, the problem of evil, the different ways faith and reason have been balanced in history, etc. But I also wanted to deal in a more concrete way with the reality of religious life and some of the passions and struggles within it and around it. I thought it would be both challenging and fun, before we attacked the standard problems, to begin with Freud's *Future of an Illusion*, to consider one view of the weakness and the harm of religion. I followed this with Thomas Merton's *Faith and Violence*, showing one person—a celibate monk, no less—doing what Freud claimed to be impossible for a believer to do: engaging the real problems of the world in a serious way.

One year, so that students might have a handy collection of religious writings, I assigned James's *The Varieties of Religious Experience*, thinking we could easily skim through some hefty chunks of it and that students would probably like both the religious variety and James himself. It turned out to be a stranger experience than I expected.

I was much more familiar with James's other work than with *The Varieties*. What I had thought to use as a simple anthology turned out to have its own insistent and unusual point of view. Students who thought of religion as church on Sunday and of religious experience as singing around a campfire or having sex weren't sure what to make of George Fox walking barefoot in winter through a river of blood. They were puzzled by how exactly something like that fit with the rest of the course, and I realized I had to struggle a bit to explain how it did. It was as though we had left the Philosophy of Religion and were studying one thinker's vision of the extreme splendors and miseries of human life. What I had meant as illustration insisted on being taken for itself, whatever that was.

I had read and enjoyed Bruce Wilshire's book *William James and Phenomenology: A Study of "The Principles of Psychology,"* where he showed how difficult it was to grasp what James was doing, how he seemed to be inventing methodologies and shifting directions as he went along. It seemed to me something like that could be done with *The Varieties*.

I was in my office one day, a windowless cell in the attic of Recitation Hall that I shared with another grad student, when one of the older philosophy professors, Richard Grabau, appeared among us, an extraordinarily rare event, asking if anyone was interested in religion.

(Now there's a phrase to ponder: "interested in religion.")

Here's what had happened:

One of Dr. Grabau's students had received a grant from a federal agency (which I'm ashamed to say I can no longer identify) to write his dissertation in the philosophy of religion. But at Purdue all such grants were modeled on research grants in the sciences: it was the professor who was given the grant, with the student working under that professor. The student had left because he'd been offered a teaching job, but Dr. Grabau could retain the grant as long as another student could come up with a proposal reasonably close to the original one.

I told him I'd been thinking about doing something on *The Varieties* and he said that was close enough for him. I should write up a proposal, he would submit it as a revision, and I could spend a couple of years getting paid to do nothing but read and write about William James. I would have said at the time I was lucky to be offered this but, looking back over a lifetime and knowing about the struggles of students today, I'd say I had no idea just how incredibly lucky and privileged I was.

I liked Dr. Grabau. He was a much less intense character than Dr. Smith, less charismatic and inspiring, but he had the gentle smile and peaceful calm of the truly wise. He spoke fluent German, taught the continental philosophers, and loved German culture, especially its music. He claimed he was offered a chance, while touring the Vatican, to play one of the organs: since he was a Lutheran, he gave them his best rendition of "A Mighty Fortress." I seem to remember him always wearing a bow tie.

I felt comfortable enough with him to throw in a few jokes in my proposal, imagining his chuckle as he edited them out. You were supposed to think up—again, on the model of the sciences—experimental work which might relate to your topic: always impatient with bureaucratic demands, I said I'd like to work with NASA to explore if mystical experiences would be possible on the moon or if they could only occur within earth's atmosphere.

The next time I ran into Dr. Grabau, I asked him, "How'd you like my moon experiment idea?"

"What moon experiment?"

"In the grant proposal. You know, where they ask you to come up with possible experiments."

"You didn't expect me to read it, did you? I just attached a note to it and sent it in." He walked away smiling, shaking his head at my naïve idea of how senior professors spend their time.

I wondered for a while if I had spoiled my chances of getting the grant approved. But we didn't get the proposal back, a testimony to either the government's sense of humor or its indifference, the money came through, and I was off to enjoy my precious gift of time to study, think, and write. (I had a lot of fun telling this story, and I still enjoy the thought of my moon experiment sleeping within some federal agency's archives, waiting for future historians to unearth it and to wonder what we were thinking in those days.)

As I said, my problems with teaching *The Varieties* had already given me a direction to explore, but I had other reasons to be pleased to be working on James. First, there was James himself: a fine writer, a delight to read, with a body of work that invited broad engagement, and a fine spirit, a character it was a pleasure to spend time with. (Anyone who's read Ray Monk's biography of Bertrand Russell and seen how, over the years of research, Monk came to loathe Russell can appreciate this.) Second, I wanted to do something in my dissertation that was a little off the beaten path. I was much more interested in grappling with a philosopher and working out what I thought in my own writing than in mastering a mountain of secondary material, an unavoidable task if you write, say, on Plato or Descartes. I suppose, in general, I enjoyed the thinking and writing more than the sheer scholarship. James was a relatively recent figure and, of his work, *The Varieties* was relatively neglected, so I could get away with indulging myself. Finally, I could avoid (almost) entirely some of the dominant orthodoxies of the time: the analytic philosophers, the logicians, and the philosophers of language who had squeezed so much life and interest and value out of the philosophical community. The Anglo-American thinkers of the twentieth century had not only narrowed philosophy's discussions: they had narrowed and hidden much of its past. Someone introduced to philosophy when I was would be surprised to learn, for example, how much Kant wrote about politics, or how much David Hume's philosophy as such was shaped by his assault on religion, how much he wrote about religion as a way of exploring knowledge itself and the human community in all its illusions. Writing on James would allow me to reenter the broader world of philosophy that first attracted me.

Thus, for many reasons, I was set to enjoy myself, and I did.

I had a fairly easy time with my dissertation committee but, as I got things in on time, wrote fairly clearly and concisely, and pretty much took suggestions agreeably, I made their lives easier, too.

I remember only a couple of things from that process.

For some reason, no doubt because I'd read so many books from England, I tended to use British rather than American spelling, e.g., "judgement" rather than "judgment." When I got back the copy of my first chapter from Dr. Grabau, I saw he had, to my astonishment, crossed out "e" in "judgement" every time it appeared. This became a kind of silent contest, never discussed: I kept using "e"; he kept eliminating it. (I would have said I had given in by the final version. But, having looked it up, I find, again to my astonishment, I did not.)

The comment from Dr. Grabau I remember most vividly is his telling me that reading my chapters was like reading detective stories: he kept waiting to come across the clue that would reveal what was going on. (It occurs to me that readers of this prologue may have a similar reaction.) He may have meant it as a complaint but I decided to take it as a compliment. Anyway, I hadn't written as I did deliberately to mystify him: it was my version of clarity, so there wasn't much I could do to change it.

The other comment I remember was from another member of my committee, William Rowe, who taught the higher-level Philosophy of Religion courses and who was far more adept at logic than I could ever be. (I have a memory of being in one of Dr. Rowe's classes that is so horrible I can't be sure it wasn't one of my nightmares—which may say something in itself about the level of intensity in grad school. I see myself standing at the blackboard trying to translate the ontological argument into the symbols of modal logic. Why I would even attempt this escapes me entirely, but my effort fell apart about halfway through and I turned to Dr. Rowe, held out the chalk, and said, "You can probably do this much better than I can." Another gentle and gracious man, Dr. Rowe laughed and took the chalk to continue, as though we were a logical tag team.)

The comment of his I remember must have come near the end of my writing. He had been telling me that I should think about working up some of my dissertation for publication and that I should have an easier time doing that than some students would, which really was a compliment. Then he said this, and it seemed as though he were trying to console me: "You know, I think everybody that writes *on* James eventually starts to write *like* James." I think he meant: too few fine distinctions, too many leaps beyond the evidence. But, again, I took it as a compliment because I could see nothing better than writing like William James.

But my strongest memory of the months and months I worked on my dissertation is the way all my days seemed to merge into one. I can't even remember writing or typing: I see myself, quite still, at a desk, in my office or the library or in our apartment, while my mind probes a world of arguments and examples and questions, an expanding world that's like an endless and fascinating maze, growing as I move through it. I remember how thrilling it was to study that seriously and intensely. I liked the energetic field a project like that becomes, striking sparks off everything in your life. The one physical memory I have is of ending the day with pockets full of notes on small scraps of paper which I'd roll up and place in the holes of an eighteen-inch pipe rack I got from my grandfather. I would do that about ten o'clock at night when I'd force myself to quit and think about something else or I would never fall asleep.

But this was more than serious study and became a serious life encounter. Or perhaps I should say: because it was serious study, because James was a great and serious philosopher, it became a serious episode in my life. James took me to the heart of philosophical questioning: What is the world like and how should we live in it? What, in the greatest sense, is going on and what should I do about it? This was a gift in itself, immediately luminous, as James might say, but it was not without practical consequences. I had grown up as a Roman Catholic but grown away from its authoritarianism, its moral bullying, its misogyny and bigotry. Part of what drew me to philosophy and to James was the freedom I saw there. I suppose *The Varieties* seemed to offer a way of being religious (in the best sense) without being religious (in the worst sense). But struggling with James and deciding he was at least partly wrong about what the world was like and what was going on in it actually sent me back to religious communities and religious traditions, away from the extreme individualism I found so attractive. It's probably no surprise that, when my hopes for a teaching career (in some small, liberal-arts version of paradise) came to nothing, I eventually spent my life as a pastor of Christian congregations in the very creed-and-doctrine-heavy, very community-centered, not-all-that-mystical Lutheran tradition.

On Religious Life: William James and I

At the time, however, I thought I would spend my working life as an academic philosopher, specializing in American studies. I thought the pragmatists and, more generally, the philosophers that were grouped around James, like Royce and Santayana, formed a coherent philosophical meditation on the modern world's mysteries and miseries, its cultural collisions, and its accelerating rate of change. I thought I could be to the pragmatists what Perry Miller was to the puritans.

I called my dissertation "William James and the Gods: A Peek at the Conceptual Underbelly of *The Varieties of Religious Experience*." When I had published the first paper I shaped from it, "Seraph, Snake and Saint: The Subconscious Mind in James' *Varieties*," in the *Journal of the American Academy of Religion*, I imagined I had laid the foundations of a life's work. This was about 1973 or 1974.

About twenty years later, I was reading an article about education in *The New York Review of Books*, and the author gave 1973 as the date the bottom fell out of the humanities job market and young scholars who had intended to teach had to begin looking for other employment. I can remember vividly the precise moment I gave up looking for a teaching job. I had already found other employment—working as a steamfitter and then as a thermostat mechanic in Purdue's maintenance department—but I was still going to philosophy conventions, applying for the same jobs several hundred other, equally or better qualified candidates were. I was sitting late one afternoon, waiting my turn to be interviewed, and I was talking to a very bright woman who said she'd had four one-year teaching positions, spread all over the country—something like Vermont to New Mexico to South Carolina to Oregon. She had now been unemployed for a year. She remarked that all she'd really been doing for five years was job hunting. That seemed to me a life not worth living, and I thought: I'm through with this. I went home, went back to my job with what James might say was an undivided self, and eventually ended up serving as a Lutheran pastor, which gave me a different way to read, write, and philosophize.

Not being an academic turned out to be its own kind of gift. I didn't spend my life studying and analyzing the philosophers I loved but living with them, enjoying them. James and his works became my companions. *The Varieties* is one of the books I've returned to every few years for enjoyment and enlightenment, like *Hamlet* and *Moby Dick*. James himself has been no less a human presence in my life than teachers I knew in the flesh, than friends and family. I remember his words; I like to imagine my choices might please him; he's one of the people I've tried to live up to. (I realize that, as I'm writing this, I'm wearing a sweatshirt with his picture on it, with the quote: "Wisdom is learning what to overlook.")

But now that I'm closer to the end of my life than to the beginning, now that I have the time in retirement to scribble away as I please, I thought I might like to make a book of my time with William James, to give his thoughts a last serious look, as a kind of grateful testimony.

Here's how this book will proceed:

Part Two is the text of a lecture I was asked to give when I was a student at Luther Northwestern Theological Seminary in St. Paul, Minnesota. I confess I gave it a ridiculous title I hoped might provoke the theologians: "Evil, Evolution, and the Creativity of Chaos: William James and the Human Plight." Much of the lecture itself now strikes me as deliberately provocative as well, but I've resisted the temptation to alter it. This was my one brief overview of James's philosophy; bearing the mark of its occasion hardly makes it unusual.

Part Three, the major portion of this work, is a deeper look back at the work of James that entered my life most deeply: *The Varieties of Religious Experience*. Having struggled to a different understanding of religious life by arguing with James, chewing over again my early work in which that argument took place will close a circle for me.

I intend this essay to be more affectionate than academic, more an act of engagement than of scholarship, so I've pretty much eliminated all references to anyone but James. I'll note in the introduction to Part Three the different things I was concerned with in this rumination, but here I must mention one general alteration of something that jarred me on almost every page of my early work, much to my surprise.

I had utterly forgotten how thoughtlessly common in that era was the use of "man," "men," "mankind," and other male terms to refer to human beings as individuals or to humanity as a whole, as well as the nearly exclusive use of "he" for God. Since then, the church I served as a pastor has made a determined and, judging by its effect on me, fairly successful effort to replace such terms with more inclusive or gender-neutral language. (I should say I regard this as an important and long overdue adjustment of the way we think about human and divine life.) I wasn't surprised that James's language had dated, because I used a passage from him once to illustrate this issue. But I was stunned at how relentlessly the male terms filled my own writing and, after a few pages, I was cringing at their appearance. I hope I've managed to eliminate them all, one way or another.

James's language, of course, I left as it was, though it too made me cringe sometimes. I'm horrified by all attempts to edit the past to make it more acceptable to our current world. One of the gifts the past can give us is its strangeness, something on its very surface to make us realize earlier thinkers really weren't just like us. (It's a minor theme of this work, of *The Varieties*, and of James's work as a whole, that all understanding shifts over time.)

In Part Four, I will gather up some of the ways James has surfaced in my life over the years and bid him farewell.

When I was working as a steamfitter, I had a friend who had been a passionate campus pastor during the Vietnam War; he'd had a serious breakdown and now also worked for Purdue's maintenance department. Whenever I'd talk too much about books, he'd quote *Ecclesiastes* to me: "Of the making of books there is no end." Mike very definitely saw that as an admonition to the truly wise, that they at least might have done with it, or at least see how small their efforts were, given all the books that are and will be out there. I grant the smallness, but I think the proverb is a recognition that we're not going to stop. We all want to keep the conversation going.

I suppose, by now, the world probably doesn't need one more book on William James. And yet . . . I think I do. So: here it is.

Part Two

Evil, Evolution, and the Creativity of Chaos: William James and the Human Plight

A lecture given to the faculty and student body of Luther Northwestern Seminary, 1982

THERE IS A STORY by Nicolai Gogol, a terrifying little tale, in which a cocky, intellectual young man returns from the university to a small peasant village. Somehow he finds himself spending a night in a haunted church with a corpse. He is armed with his intellect and his courage and one piece of good advice: he will be safe so long as he keeps from looking at the monsters that haunt the church. He goes; and in the middle of the night a whirlwind sweeps the nave, the windows smash, the icons fall on their faces, and a whole horde of horrors, scratching claws and swishing wings, swoop in, searching for the human they can sense.

The young man remembers his advice. He keeps his eyes tightly shut. But finally his curiosity overcomes him, and he looks up at the great beast.

"*There* he is!" it shrieks.

And all the screaming monsters, great and small, pounce on him and destroy him.

All great philosophers are like that young man. Cocky, skeptical, courageous, they squat amid the wreckage of ancient beliefs. And they can't resist looking the monsters right in the eye, whatever it costs.

I was asked to speak to you this morning about one such philosopher: William James. Rather than give the rather obvious theological critique of his leading ideas or try to relate him to parish life, that last great measure of relevance, I want to give you the "particular *go*," as he would say, of his philosophy, make you see what made him tick, who he was, and why you should be interested in him.

William James was not, I think, related to those celebrated princes of outlawry, Frank and Jesse, but his fate in our culture has not been unlike theirs: spurned, because feared, by institutions and established powers, yet dearly loved by common folk, and finally so richly *there* that assimilation and veneration became necessary.

He *was* related to an even more extraordinary James family, most of whom were artistic geniuses, alcoholics, visionaries, neurotics, or several of those things together. William said that his brother Henry, the great novelist, was "a native of the James family and has no other country." That was certainly true of William and most of the others. For several generations, they all seemed to be named Henry, William, or Alice, until Henry the novelist complained that the James children had to spend most of their time wondering which one they were.

William's father, Henry Sr, was a restless mystical writer who travelled constantly, dragging his family with him. William crossed the Atlantic six times before he was nineteen (and many times after). When he was older and famous, and was asked to lecture on education, he characterized the educated person this way: "one who is . . . able practically to extricate himself . . . from circumstances in which he never was placed before."[1] He didn't mean it as a joke. Being educated means being able to get out of traps (a militant vision, of which I shall say more later).

William's dates are 1842–1910 and he seems so modern when you read him that it is a shock to realize that his *younger* brothers fought in the Civil War. He came to philosophy very late. In fact, he held his first job when he was 30 and was married only at thirty-six (to a woman named, of course, Alice, who looked rather like Burt Lancaster). He seemed to start a new career every ten years, moving from painting to medicine to psychology, finally writing—almost in spite of himself—some classic philosophical works: *The Will to Believe*, *Pragmatism*, *A Pluralistic Universe* (whose titles and themes are often used to describe American society), and two great books: *The Principles of Psychology* and *The Varieties of Religious Experience*.

But what explains this hesitation and restlessness and drives him through the books and themes he develops is that he was, through and

---

1. James, *Writings 1878–1899*, 730.

Evil, Evolution, and the Creativity of Chaos

through, a religious thinker, a pilgrim, looking for a new Jerusalem his world was no longer able to define.

James wanted to be Emerson, the minister who left the pulpit but preached his whole life. What he became was a doctor who never practiced medicine yet spent his whole life trying to heal, primarily himself. He was a spiritual pilgrim, and the wilderness he was lost in was the modern world.

Someone said that James was always a charming, vibrant companion but that whenever you met him he seemed to step out of some great sadness into which, when you left him, he would step back again. Sadness, despair, loss and lostness—that's the "go" of James's thought. Evil was the one thing he was impressed with above all others, evil personal and social, natural and moral. Intellectually, living when he did, his thought was pulled into the orbit of evolution. But his distinctive value as a thinker was that he looked for solace and solution not apart from but right in the wilderness that evil and evolution defined, in the chaos and its promise of creativity. Instead of running from the monsters, he looked them right in the eye. That's the curve of his thought that I'd like to impress you with.

"In the deepest heart of all of us," James wrote, "there is a corner in which the ultimate mystery of things works sadly,"[2] where during "the hour of terror at the world's vast meaningless grinding"[3] one felt "the blighting breath of the ultimate Why?"[4] There was a terror he found written across the whole human world: "That life is not worth living the whole army of suicides declare—an army whose roll-call, like the famous evening gun of the British army, follows the sun round the world and never terminates."[5]

James had discovered this corner in himself early in life. In his lectures on religious experience, he presented his own story as the story of a friend, but it came from his diary when he was twenty-seven:

> Whilst in this state of philosophic pessimism and general depression of spirits about my prospects, I went one evening into a dressing-room in the twilight to procure some article that was there; when suddenly there fell upon me without any warning, just as if it came out of the darkness, a horrible fear of my own existence. Simultaneously there arose in my mind the image of an epileptic patient whom I had seen in the asylum, a black-haired youth with

---

2. Ibid., 480.
3. Ibid., 587.
4. Ibid., 511.
5. Ibid., 484.

greenish skin, entirely idiotic, who used to sit all day on one of the benches ... with his knees drawn up against his chin, and the coarse gray undershirt, which was his only garment, drawn over them inclosing his entire figure. He sat there like a sort of sculptured Egyptian cat or Peruvian mummy, moving nothing but his black eyes and looking absolutely non-human. This image and my fear entered into a species of combination with each other. *That shape am I,* I felt, potentially. Nothing that I possess can defend me against that fate, if the hour for it should strike for me as it struck for him. There was such a horror of him, and such a perception of my own merely momentary discrepancy from him, that it was as if something hitherto solid within my breast gave way entirely, and I became a mass of quivering fear.[6]

He was in this condition for months, and he says: "I remember wondering how other people could live, how I myself had ever lived, so unconscious of that pit of insecurity beneath the surface of life."[7]

He used this experience as an avenue for exploring the shape of the world and found a wrongness, an unease at its very heart: "No easy fine, no mere apology or formal expiation, will satisfy the world's demands, but every pound of flesh exacted is soaked with all its blood."[8] "The lunatic's visions of horror are all drawn from the material of daily fact. Our civilization is founded on the shambles, and every individual existence goes out in a lonely spasm of helpless agony";[9] . . . "desperation absolute and complete, the whole universe coagulating about the sufferer into a material of overwhelming horror, surrounding him without opening or end. Not the conception or intellectual perception of evil, but the grisly blood-freezing heart-palsying sensation of it close upon one, and no other conception or sensation able to live for a moment in its presence."[10]

"Here is the real core of the religious problem: Help! help! No prophet can claim to bring a final message unless he says things that will have a sound of reality in the ears of victims such as these."[11]

That was the look of things for James. And the absence of messages tuned to his ears astounded him.

6. James, *Writings 1902–1910,* 149–50.
7. Ibid., 150.
8. Ibid., 130.
9. Ibid., 152.
10. Ibid., 151.
11. Ibid.

Evil, Evolution, and the Creativity of Chaos

Every generation has scientists, whose good will—says James—exceeds their perspicacity, who rave about the glorious plan of nature. But what do we actually find in nature?

> Beauty and hideousness, love and cruelty, life and death keep house together in indissoluble partnership; and there gradually stands over us, instead of the old warm notion of a man-loving Deity, that of an awful power that neither hates nor loves, but rolls all things together meaninglessly to a common doom.[12]

Theologians and philosophers like to talk about evil finding its explanation in the higher purposes of God. This makes sense in some particular cases. Stub your toe—well, watch your step. But, on the whole, "the scale of the evil actually in sight defies all human tolerance. . . . A God who can relish such superfluities of horror is no God for human beings to appeal to. His animal spirits are too high."[13]

This is the voice of the religious rebel, of Ivan Karamazov, of Camus, the voice of the person who *will not* believe because such a submission would be outrageous. And James knows that the impulse behind this rebellion is still religious, "the sick shudder of the frustrated religious demand."[14] "That is why I call Pessimism an essentially religious disease."[15] It is *both* the desire, the need for perfection, wholeness, salvation, *and* the obvious lack of it in the world that yields this poisonous, nightmarish view.[16]

Though he had great respect for Christianity and its history, the Christianity of his own place and time gave him little help: "We have now whole congregations whose preachers, far from magnifying our consciousness of sin, seem devoted rather to making little of it. They ignore, or even deny, eternal punishment, and insist on the dignity rather than on the depravity of man. . . . a sanguine and 'muscular' attitude, which to our forefathers would have seemed purely heathen, has become in their eyes an ideal element of Christian character."[17]

James had his own distaste for theories of eternal punishment, but they at least bespoke a seriousness of religion, and he agreed with Emerson who said that "Luther . . . would have cut off his right hand rather than

---

12. James, *Writings 1878–1899*, 487.
13. James, *Writings 1902–1910*, 548.
14. James, *Writings 1878–1899*, 488.
15. Ibid., 486.
16. Ibid., 487–88.
17. James, *Writings 1902–1910*, 88.

nail his theses to the door at Wittenberg, if he had supposed that they were destined to lead to the pale negations of Boston Unitarianism."[18]

Like the young Luther, James had his despair intensified by reigning systems of thought that seemed to make action pointless and banish hope even further. For James, those systems of thought were the popular scientific philosophies of the nineteenth century, which were loosely based on a materialistic reading of Darwin. James variously labeled these naturalism, evolutionism, Darwinism, and he set his writings in dialogue primarily with thinkers like Spencer, Huxley, Clifford—people who constructed supposedly scientific philosophies. Like the cold touch of the lunatic's vision, these philosophies seemed to James to yield only a spiritual paralysis. With their materialism and their determinism, they offered no motive for action, destroying any point to conduct, every ground of hope.

Take our common experiences, says James (and as we have seen, these can be bleak enough) and

> place round them . . . the curdling cold and gloom and absence of all permanent meaning which for pure naturalism and the popular science evolutionism of our time are all that is visible ultimately, and the thrill [of life] stops short, or turns rather to an anxious trembling.
>
> For naturalism, fed on recent cosmological speculations, mankind is in a position similar to that of a set of people living on a frozen lake, surrounded by cliffs over which there is no escape, yet knowing that little by little the ice is melting, and the inevitable day drawing near when the last film of it will disappear, and to be drowned ignominiously will be the human creature's portion.[19]

As much as any religious fatalism, naturalism presented James with a block universe, with all of its parts in a death embrace, making action pointless and escape impossible.

Now here was a trap, and a grim one. James got out not by looking for some fixed place to plant his feet—such as papal infallibility or the literal inspiration of scripture, popular solutions of the time—but by plunging deeper into the chaos. (He wrote once: "even in the pessimistically-tending mind . . . where the loving and admiring impulses are dead, the hating and fighting impulses will still respond to fit appeals."[20]) James went back to

---

18. Ibid., 302.
19. Ibid., 133.
20. James, *Writings 1878–1899*, 491.

Darwin's writings themselves to beat the philosophies of the day with their own weapons. And it is impossible to overstate how liberating he found Darwin to be.

Of course, one could see in Darwin the bleakness, the struggle, the materialism, but what James saw was change, movement, freedom, nature in motion, creation unended and unending, and the appearance in nature of "spontaneous variations" that brought new qualities into existence.

Darwin had distinguished between the production of an organism, its appearance, and its maintenance of survival; the theory of natural selection was formed to explain the latter. James, however, fastened on the mere *fact* of the former, the appearance of variations, as nature's great offering of novelty, a living sign of creation and possibility, the gift of a future. He applied it to every arena of natural and cultural life, seeing ideas, ideals, and even great individuals as "spontaneous variations" in their respective environments.

The world was not a frozen lake. New things could happen. This was the thread James grasped and he never let go of it. And now his philosophical quest took clearer shape. He would show that the world was less of a block and more of a chaotic mess, and that that was good. He would show that we were less spectators and more acting, desiring organisms, and that that was good. And he would show that the true locus of religious, philosophical, social, and natural arbitration was neither present evidence nor past custom but the future shape of things, as yet unsettled, and that that was good.

The unsettledness, the chaos, is the key that turned James around, the key that he wants to use to turn us, from ourselves and our frozen predicament, into the future. "All these ultimate questions," he says, "turn, as it were upon their hinges.... The really vital question for us all is, What is this world going to be? What is life eventually to make of itself? The centre of gravity of philosophy must therefore alter its place.... It will be an alteration in 'the seat of authority' that reminds one almost of the protestant reformation."[21]

This quest is the nerve of his philosophies of pragmatism and pluralism. (And I think you can see that it does have an American tone: there is a faith in dissolving powers, the acids of conflict and revolution, there is an obsession with action and struggle, and there is a bright and wild-eyed gaze at the future. But I hope you also see that it began in a deep spiritual

---

21. James, *Writings 1902–1910*, 540.

dis-ease and was forged in intimate dialogue with broader religious and scientific traditions.)

So the primary thing he set out to do was turn us back into the chaos. The problem with all our systems of thought, our social institutions, our identities, is that they hide that chaos and flux of life. He says, "All our scientific and philosophic ideals are altars to unknown gods."[22] Like the Apostle Paul, James thought he knew how, why, and to whom those altars were built. And the great part of his thought is directed at replacing us in the bubbling caldron of experience out of which such things are cooked up. He loved to talk about what he thought was the life of primitive cultures but which was really his own vision of our true experience:

> Nature can have little unity for savages. It is a Walpurgis-nacht procession, a checkered play of light and shadow, a medley of impish and elfish friendly and inimical powers. . . . If a bit of cosmic emotion ever thrills them, it is likely to be at midnight, when the camp smoke rises straight to the wicked full moon in the zenith, and the forest is all whispering with witchery and danger. The eeriness of the world, the mischief and the manyness, the littleness of the forces, the magical surprises, the unaccountability of every agent, . . . these communicate the thrills of curiosity and the earliest intellectual strivings. Tempests and conflagrations, pestilences and earthquakes, reveal supramundane powers, and instigate religious terror rather than philosophy. Nature, more demonic than divine, is above all things *multifarious*. So many creatures that feed or threaten, that help or crush, so many beings to love or hate, to understand or start at—which is on top or which subordinate? Who can tell?[23]

James wants to see everything under the sun—tigers, plants, governments, and ideals—as part of this dance of nature. He isn't interested in making a lot of distinctions between nature, society, personality. And while ideals and institutions introduce order into the chaos (he admits that), they do so at some cost. (That's what he wants everybody else to admit.) This is what he means by pluralism: the multifariousness of the world and the uneasiness of the way things fit and refuse to fit together. He did not mean, as Mr. Rogers does, "everyone has a point of view and isn't that nice?" He meant everything and everyone had a unique shape and sometimes they fit but sometimes they didn't and that meant a good deal of suffering but,

22. James, *Writings 1878–1899*, 568.
23. James, *Writings 1902–1910*, 639–40.

Evil, Evolution, and the Creativity of Chaos

thank God and nature, things are sloppy enough that the last word is still to be said. Applying this vision to the moral life, he says:

> The pinch is always here. Pent in under every system of moral rules are innumerable persons whom it weighs upon, and goods which it represses: and these are always rumbling and grumbling in the background, and ready for any issue by which they may get free. See the abuses which the institution of private property covers, so that even today it is shamelessly asserted among us, that one of the prime functions of the national government is to help the adroiter citizens to grow rich. See the unnamed and unnameable sorrows which the tyranny, on the whole so beneficent, of the marriage-institution brings to so many, both of the married and the unwed. . . . See everywhere the struggle and the squeeze; and everlastingly the problem how to make them less.[24]

Nature and morality, society and divinity—all were part of one grand struggle for James.

And armed with this vision, he was able to redefine human beings, seeing them not as paralyzed spectators, dispassionate knowers of a finished world, but as participating animals, part of nature, actors in its struggle. This is what he means by pragmatism.

James sometimes felt there was a conspiracy to willfully misunderstand everything he said about pragmatism. I'm convinced he was right. "Pragmatic" is usually taken as a synonym for "thoughtless activity" or "expediency." I find it somewhat droll, though not surprising, that the Marxist term *praxis* should have such a high standing for some theologians. Using a different form of the same Greek root and appealing to a German rather than an American thinker strikes one as unimpressive. It's probably that continental "ah" in *praxis* that seems so much more sophisticated than the Yankee "eeh" in "pragmatism."

James never meant that acting is important *and thinking isn't* or that *nothing but* action *really* mattered (though his interests and examples tended this way). Rather, he wanted to redefine everything human beings were involved in as a kind of action. Thus, thinking was a kind of action, feeling was a kind of action, art and philosophy were kinds of action. Activity became for James what first willing was and now speaking is for Ricoeur, and what perception was for Merleau-Ponty, an avenue for understanding our

---

24. James, *Writings 1878–1899*, 611–12.

place in the world, something that bridged the discontinuity of experience between mind and body, self and world.

He saw the human being as a complex arc of response to the world—beginning in some definite situation and reaching back into the world, into the future, an *acting* organism. And because this arc ran through the marvelous human personality, it was no mechanical response he saw but a teleological one; it reached toward some purpose, some goal, however vague.

This brings one to the second thing James didn't mean by "pragmatic": when he said truth is "what works" he didn't mean what was expedient in the short term. He had in mind this reach into the future. He meant that after we've considered present evidence and past tradition in any endeavor—scientific, moral, religious—there is still one vital question to ask about our theories and beliefs: What promise do they hold for the future? That is the question turning on its hinges and it is a question that involves not only our knowledge but our desires and our hopes as well. That is pragmatism: understanding the whole of life as activity, activity reaching into the future.

And any belief that blunts that reach—as naturalism did for James, as pessimism did, as determinism and atheism did—can be rejected for that very reason. And any belief that sharpens that reach—as religious beliefs of all sorts do—can be held for that reason.

Again you can see the mark of the theory of evolution: James respects the deepest yearnings of all organisms, and for human beings he thought that meant their religious yearnings. That organic yearning is what sets James's doctrine of the will-to-believe apart from simply irrational and voluntaristic beliefs or intellectual challenges like Pascal's wager. The human heart with a need for God—Augustine, Freud, and James all acknowledged the need. Augustine had no problems seeing the roots of the knowledge of God there; Freud thought it was an illusion, however deep. And James—James thought the human heart deserved to take its shot.

He thought every human heart deserved it though he knew too well that we had not one yearning but a whole "howling mob of desires, each struggling to get breathing room for the ideal to which it clings"[25] He knew that all desires *could not* share a common life, however wide we stretch the future: "Some part of the ideal must be butchered.... It is a tragic situation, and no mere speculative conundrum."[26]

---

25. Ibid., 609.
26. Ibid.

Yet the cardinal virtue of this philosophy is tolerance: "Everybody," James laments, "remains outside of everybody else's sight."[27] And though we cannot share or live with everyone's yearnings, we can at least understand them, significantly—in this philosophy of action—by seeing them as a struggle: "The solid meaning of life is always the same eternal thing—the marriage, namely, of some unhabitual ideal, however special, with fidelity, courage, and endurance; with some man's or woman's pains."[28] And that buys James's respect.

In the vision of liberal society, the arenas of arbitration for conflicting desires are the courts and the assemblies and their ringmaster is the politician. For James, arbitration comes in the hard court of the pitiless future and its officers are the saints and the freaks, those who can inspire others to share their larger visions (something that maybe is not so irrelevant to parish ministry):

> Only in some pitiful dreamer, some philosopher, poet, or romancer, or when the common practical man becomes a lover, does the hard externality give way, and a gleam of insight into . . . the vast world of inner life beyond us, so different from that of outer seeming, illuminate our mind. Then the whole scheme of our customary values gets confounded, then our self is riven and its narrow interests fly to pieces, then a new centre and a new perspective must be found.[29]

> The saints, with their extravagance of human tenderness are the great torchbearers . . . , the tip of the wedge, the cleavers of the darkness.[30]

Which vision will finally shape the world is still in doubt; the here and now is a struggle of conflicting visions, which was fine with James.

A friend of his once told him that the thought of such a universe as he described "made him sick, like the sight of the horrible motion of a mass of maggots in their carrion bed."[31]

To things like this, James replied,

---

27. Ibid., 878.
28. Ibid.
29. Ibid., 847.
30. James, *Writings 1902–1910*, 325.
31. James, *Writings 1878–1899*, 590.

> In this real world of sweat and dirt, it seems to me that when a view of things is "noble"' that ought to count as a presumption against its truth, and as a philosophic disqualification. The prince of darkness may be a gentleman, as we are told he is, but whatever the God of earth and heaven is, he can surely be no gentleman. His menial services are needed in the dust of our human trials, even more than his dignity is needed in the empyrean.[32]

We need a God like that. And a God like that needs us. This is the last patch of ice in James's slippery vision. He sees the gods and us as partners, standing by one another if and when we share the same ideals. "The gods we stand by are the gods we need and can use, the gods whose demands on us are reinforcements of our demands on ourselves and on one another."[33] "By obstinately believing that there are gods . . . we are doing the universe the deepest service we can"[34] because we help bring to shape the things we care about. For James, God was only first among equals, the universe was "a sort of joint-stock society . . . in which the sharers have both limited liabilities and limited powers."[35]

God for William James was a kind of bigger William James, offering the promise that someone larger might care about his cares. A God who didn't, or who cared so strangely that no help came, simply did not interest James. In this "half-wild, half-saved universe,"[36] this "only partly hospitable globe,"[37] James wanted half a chance in the fight—which is just what he gave himself.

On his tortured quest, he found faith and hope—not, I think, love. Most of his metaphors are of force, his examples of battles, massacres, daring escapes. He is one of those American artists who distrust culture and society, who have no imaginative interest in either, though their gifts are precisely cultural and social, and whose moral paralysis is only cured by struggle. Like Mark Twain, Francis Parkman, Hemingway, John Huston, Norman Mailer, Sam Peckinpah—the list is as long as American history—James finally only made sense of life as a fight. He shared that alluring American nightmare of lonely battles in meaningless places.

---

32. James, *Writings 1902–1910*, 518.
33. Ibid., 303.
34. James, *Writings 1878–1899*, 476.
35. Ibid., 573.
36. Ibid., 502.
37. James, *Writings 1902–1910*, 1290.

He thought this was just true to the facts. But he also knew it was the only thing that awakened his interest in going on, the *chance* that life was not a frozen lake but a spiritual battlefield with the *chance* of victory.

He once imagined God making us this offer before creation:

> I am going to make a world not certain to be saved, a world the perfection of which shall be conditional merely, the condition being that each several agent does its own "level best." I offer you the chance of taking part in such a world. Its safety, you see, is unwarranted. It is a real adventure, with real danger, yet it may win through. It is a social scheme of cooperative work genuinely to be done. Will you join the procession? Will you trust yourself and trust the other agents enough to face the risk?[38]

And William James, the sad, lonely philosopher with the Yankee swagger, answered, like Molly Bloom, "Yes. You bet. Yes."

That's who William James was.

---

38. Ibid., 614.

Part Three

William James and the Gods (Revisited)
A(nother) Peek at the Conceptual Underbelly of *The Varieties of Religious Experience*

1. Introduction(s), Then and Now

Now I would like to chew over again my youthful engagement with *The Varieties of Religious Experience*. But first a pair of introductions.

THEN

1/ (This is what I wrote forty years ago:) Every great work produces its own caricature. Its darkest lines come to stand for its entire substance. Read such a book quickly, forget most of it, vulgarize the rest, and you have the image by which it will survive in the popular mind and the common encyclopedia article. The image of *The Varieties* goes something like this: "James begins by saying he will deal with individuals, not institutions, which is fine because all the institutions are corrupt anyway; next, he gives about three hundred pages of psychological data; finally, he concludes by saying that you can believe whatever you like." In other words, *The Varieties* has been taken as a reissue of *The Will to Believe*—with pictures.

Most discussions of James treat this marvelous book as just that: a picture book to be pillaged for the sake of illustrating arguments and positions in James's other books. I have reversed this tradition. In the following essay, I have stayed close to *The Varieties*, trying to uncover the main lines of its argument instead of placing it within the larger horizon of James's philosophy, bringing in his other works only when necessary. In a work devoted to James and religion, I have committed the unpardonable sin of not discussing the "will-to-believe" argument in detail. I am not claiming that philosophical works are best understood in isolation, merely that *The Varieties* has been obscured by its lack of isolation. The book has been taken as obviously right or obviously wrong, depending on what one thinks of James. It deserves its own reading.

It deserves an analysis, not a prose poem. James, who wrote that "technical writing on *philosophical* subjects . . . is certainly a crime against the human race!" (how can you footnote a quotation like that?), certainly discourages sober analysis. He moves most commentators to songs of praise. Though it is difficult for one who is sympathetic to James to resist this temptation, I have done my best. As Spinoza did in such a magnificent way for Descartes, I have tried to reorder the movement of James's argument. Instead of following the natural movements of a mind thinking itself into its subject, I have blocked out a number of problems that arise from a careful reading of *The Varieties*, pulled apart issues that James addressed as one, and constructed arguments and defenses out of unconnected passages. In short, I have crushed the life out of the book, created difficulties where none were before, and forced a work of passion into a cold framework of reason.

I have not done this because my heart is made of stone. I have simply tried to clarify a work that has, in fact, contributed to its own neglect by its power and the charm of its language. There are deep problems with *The Varieties*, deep confusions beneath the clear prose. But the confusions are never complete and the arguments, though submerged, can often be found.

In the first part of the essay, I have analyzed James's *approach* to religion: his conception of the religious life and religious belief, and the tools he employs in his inquiry. In the second part, I have dealt with James's *evaluation* of religion: his standards for judging it, his conclusions as to its truth and worth.

In other words, I have not, like many commentators, tried to reproduce *The Varieties*. Such an enterprise is both foolish and worthless. There is no point in wasting paper to do something done so many times, first and best of all by James himself. I have taken a—long overdue, I think—peek at the conceptual underbelly of the work. It is a book that seems to be ripped out of life and hurled on to paper with little concern for the niceties of argument. It is a book in, with, and by which one can live. The following essay is no more than an academic shoehorn but, I hope, a useful one.

NOW

2/ Now, half a lifetime later, in not only a new century but a new millennium, rereading what I wrote so long ago, I blush to see that I compared myself to Spinoza and cringe a little at what I knew even then to be an inaccurate comparison. (I think I was just showing off my knowledge of a tiny corner of philosophical history. Not, I might add, for the only time in this writing.) Beyond this, however, I find my original introduction both clear as to my intention and accurate to its execution. Reading *The Varieties* is a slippery experience because of its conceptual fuzziness and James's tendency to glide cheerfully over difficulties. He writes so engagingly you're happy to slip along with him, as you're happy letting a clever magician distract you. But a haze begins to thicken on the general landscape and, while you continue to enjoy the ride, you're not really sure where you're going or why you're going there. I think what I did in my analysis helps very much to make *The Varieties* make sense.

I was pleasantly surprised at the doggedness of my youthful self: revealing difficulties, exploring tensions and gaps in logic, putting James's book on the rack and forcing distinctions out of it. It brought back to me how hard I was trying to please Dr. Rowe. I was also very surprised at the number of sarcastic contemporary references I made: for example, when I discussed what sense it made to speak of the "same" emotion in different contexts, I compared the wrath of Daniel Berrigan, the fiery antiwar Jesuit, with the wrath of Spiro Agnew, the criminal fool who was Nixon's vice-president; at another point, I said someone who was trying to claim James as a defender of the drug culture "was unworthy to check James's books out of the library"; and I had entirely forgotten I thanked my lawyer, in the acknowledgments, for keeping me out of jail, since I wrote this work while under federal indictment for refusing induction into the armed forces.

What I want to do in this rumination is clarify my argument, and this will partly involve making it less of a Tract for the Times. I also want to purge it of the many references to the contemporary philosophical literature and the running debates in the philosophy of religion. I wasn't at all surprised to find these, since that's what the academic game involves. Some of this material, I again must confess, seems to be there only to show how much I knew, but that's part of the game, too. I'd like to free my several lines of thought from these, to make them stand out more clearly.

What I hope I've produced is what biblical scholars might call a later, (hopefully) more readable redaction of an earlier text, by an older follower of the original author.

I had attended, as a young scholar, to the conceptual structure of the book. After many rereadings over many years, I would now say that the very nature of the book is almost as hidden as the conceptual structure is. *The Varieties* purports to be a set of academic lectures on the subject of religion. But it can be seen as a story, a story filled with other stories, a philosophical *Canterbury Tales*. There are stories of the blessed and the tormented, the suffering and the saved, and there is the story of James himself, searching for something of value among the passions and the miracles.

He's searching for a different story to tell about the world, more inclusive than any one religion can tell. His saved sinners, mystics and saints are not so much examples of religious life as of life itself, come to inspire the church of all of us.

The Varieties could be taken as James's book on ethics, his book of virtue: tales of the virtuous life, with vivid illustrations of triumph and failure, bound together by a voice of tolerance. It's a book of wonder, a tour of human nature, with James pointing out the highlights, amazed at our extremes, admiring our efforts.

I hope I have made this aspect of *The Varieties* a bit more clear as well.

There's something else that strikes me now when I revisit *The Varieties* or my work on it, but it has to do more with the fortunes of religion itself in the years that have passed. James wrote and I wrote about him during times when religion could be seen as a waning power in the world, stripped of political force and the instruments of violence, more mindful of human needs and bonds than of jealous gods and human divisions. It was easy and easily provocative for James to ridicule the pale mildness of Unitarianism: he was safely distant from the reality of witch hunting and witch burning, from the savageness of religious wars. It was easy for me, growing up with the expansive ecumenical impulses that followed World War II, with the Civil Rights movement and the voices of peace condemning the Vietnam War, to think all religious impulses had been purified. It was easy for both of us to celebrate the farther reaches of religious passion, to argue for a greater place for religious life, since its place had come to seem so safely small. It was easy for two fairly secularized scholars, living fairly protected lives, to be fooled this way.

Since then, an ugly, intolerant tribalism has returned to the religions of the world and reawakened the old lust for earthly power. Women are again tortured and killed in the name of God. We can watch videos of self-proclaimed Muslims beheading infidels. Self-proclaimed Christians in America murder doctors who perform abortions. When the United States invaded Iraq, there was no shortage of Christian leaders who proclaimed it a Christian crusade and no shortage of Muslim leaders who saw it that way. Life in the city of Jerusalem can hardly be described without speaking of religious hatred and indiscriminate violence. Not that long ago, the same was true of life in Belfast. In America, as I write, there are people who seriously believe President Barack Obama is the Antichrist.

All of this has caused me to rethink James's evaluation of religion and to qualify some of the things I wrote about the value of saintliness. Still, since James hated both cruelty and intolerance, there's little doubt of what he would think about the cruelty spawned by the poisonous dogmatisms now plaguing our time.

2. The Use and Abuse of Psychology

William James, with his typical generosity and his fascination with human lives, steps aside for much of *The Varieties* and lets the people of his book tell their own stories in their own voices. It's this choir of witnesses, describing and reflecting on what they consider their deepest and most overwhelming experiences, that gives James's book its characteristic shape and flavor and provides its most lasting impression.

It's a democratic choir. James summons up the world-famous—Tolstoi, Goethe, and Whitman; the official saints—Augustine, Teresa, and Loyola; the tormented—John Bunyan and George Fox; the reflective—Edwards and Emerson, and then calls up around them, page after page, the little known and the unnamed that fill out the body of every choir and every church, finding room for those like Billy Bray, whose one foot seemed to say "Glory" and the other foot "Amen" as he walked along.[1] Even the scoffers, like Voltaire and Nietzsche, are allowed to speak for themselves.

---

1. James, *Writings 1902–1910*, 236.

He can't ever let them go. When he reaches the concluding theoretical sections of his book, he keeps apologizing for getting nowhere and seems to lose interest. The reader of *The Varieties* will be struck by how the footnotes begin to swell in this section. One James goes on lecturing while another James seems to be bored by the abstractions and begins quoting in a whisper more voices you really must hear to freshen your memory or simply to spice up what's going on. (Hidden away in a lengthy note on anaesthetics and mysticism, someone with the wonderful name of Xenos Clark says, "[T]here's a smile upon the face of the revelation. . . . 'You could kiss your own lips, and have all the fun to yourself,' it says, if you only knew the trick."[2])

The never stopping murmur of the voices becomes a kind of living background, like mumbled prayers in a church.

This is James's way of approaching his subject and of keeping life in it, but it's also much of what it means to James to say he approaches religion as a psychologist. It's a way for him to repopulate speculation and to set himself off from "philosophy," understood as a severely abstract discipline, more interested in logic than living drama. I would include, in this sense of what a psychologist offers, James's determination to push the boundaries of polite and civilized views of human nature. (Why else begin a lecture series established to explore natural theology, that most polite of religious manifestations, with George Fox wading through a stream of blood?) Even with his tamer examples, he wants to catch the peculiar richness of each individual: after introducing Whitman as a specimen of healthy-minded optimism, he spends several pages pointing out that Whitman was neither as natural nor as optimistic as he's sometimes made out to be.[3]

This is not all James means—or thinks he should mean—by "psychology," but it's important to insist on this much at the start, because of both the distortions and prejudices the term itself can call up and the strange twists and confusions of James's own procedures.

Consider this passage from *The Meaning of Truth*, where James is trying to refute the criticism that he confounds psychology with logic:

> A while ago a prisoner, on being released, tried to assassinate the judge who had sentenced him. He had apparently succeeded in conceiving the judge timelessly, had reduced him to a bare logical meaning, that of being his "enemy and persecutor," by stripping

2. Ibid., 351.
3. Ibid., 83–85.

off all the concrete conditions (as jury's verdict, official obligation, absence of personal spite, possibly sympathy) that gave its full psychological character to the sentence as a particular man's act in time.[4]

Here he equates "full psychological character" with "all the concrete conditions." The "logical" meaning is "simply the 'psychological' one disemboweled of its fullness, and reduced to a bare abstractional scheme."[5] It's tempting to say that, for James, the logical meaning is at best illusory and at worst simply false: but there's nothing *special* in the meaning of "psychology" here that would imply anything about a method of study, beyond an attempt to spell out "all the concrete conditions." What leads to some of the confusions early on in *The Varieties* is that James states there that his psychological standpoint does dictate the shape and limits of his inquiry, yet the explicit standpoint he defends doesn't play much of a role in his explorations and is more misleading than helpful.

He begins by declaring that, since his inquiry is psychological, he must deal with religious feelings and religious impulses rather than religious institutions.[6] Change the term "institutions" to "communities" or "gatherings of believers" and you might wonder how necessary this focus must be for a psychologist. In fact, the choice to concentrate on individuals rather than "institutions" is less a limitation dictated by a discipline and more a judgment by James that the real nature and truth of religion lies within believing individuals. (I'll explore this further in section four.) I think anyone who knows anything about William James wouldn't expect anything else.

But suppose we ask: James aside, what might we expect something calling itself a "psychological study of religion" to be? It's easy to think of things we would not expect to find: a logical evaluation of the ontological argument, say, or a defense of a particular creed, though we might find discussions of the motives behind them or the temperaments they appeal to. Already, we can see *The Varieties* offers something more than this, since an essential stage of the book's argument is devoted to an evaluation of the truth claims of both mysticism and philosophy; it also involves a defense, though a guarded and good-natured one, of some beliefs over others. But we do find—as we would expect—extensive discussions of conversion experiences, alleged encounters with spiritual powers, etc. Would we expect

4. Ibid., 905.
5. Ibid., 904.
6. Ibid., 12.

to find references to alcoholism and drug-induced trances? Perhaps. Such discussions *are* in *The Varieties*, however small is the space devoted to them. But their mere presence raises the issue acutely: beyond a focus on individuals, what does James think the psychological study of religion involves?

He begins by distinguishing two orders of inquiry concerning anything: "First, what is the nature of it? how did it come about? what is its constitution, origin and history? And second, what is its importance, meaning, or significance, now that it is once here?"[7] This is his distinction between an *existential* judgment—the determination of a thing's origins, its causes—and a *spiritual* judgment—the value of a thing in itself. This seems, at first, straightforward enough: someone might admit the Bible was written by humans, yet still find it valuable as a guide to life; math and science departments might be partially funded by the Department of Defense, but their research could still be solid. The main point he wants to make is that simply to ascertain the origin of a thing is not yet to ascertain its value. Things get complicated, however, when a particular origin seems by itself to discredit a thing's value: political parties spend a great deal of energy trying to hide the source of their own funding and reveal the source of their opponent's funding because the money itself implies a strong bias and makes policies and decisions suspect; for fundamentalists, accepting that the Bible is of human origin means the end of faith.

James still wants us to realize that there are two distinct judgments being made; but, in such cases, the origin is functioning as at least part of the spiritual judgment of value, in different ways. (James argues that this is simply an easy way of taking care of our spiritual judgments: deducing value from origin, which then functions as a dogmatic standard.[8])

This distinction is important for James because what he sees himself bringing as a psychologist will simply amount to considering religious phenomena "from the purely existential point of view."[9] The distinction is thus a kind of self-defense, allaying the fears of his audience that his standpoint, by itself, might completely discredit all things religious. But the problems begin when James goes into detail about what this apparently tidy distinction involves.

For the existential judgment, there are two tasks: classification and causal explanation. "The first thing the intellect does with an object is to

7. Ibid., 13.
8. Ibid., 25.
9. Ibid., 14.

class it along with something else."[10] Since the inquiry will deal with religious individuals "for whom religion exists not as a dull habit, but as an acute fever,"[11] we will be dealing with people who approach the pathological; they see visions, feel themselves moved physically by superior powers and exhibit symptoms of nervous instability. Thus, a psychologist taking the existential point of view will treat these pathological aspects of religion as instances of certain kinds of human feelings, "just as if they occurred in non-religious men."[12] (There is an obvious problem in saying the "same" experience occurs in both religious and nonreligious people; we will return to this. To anticipate, I would say this is another example of James's execution happily ignoring his stated intention.)

"The next thing the intellect does is to lay bare the causes in which the thing originates."[13] Ultimately, this might involve a decision about the reality of the supernatural beings or powers claimed to be experienced; and this is perhaps the most elusive question in *The Varieties*. James wants to say that even if we concluded religious experiences were caused by miserable diets, the question of value would still be open. This is the very sort of claim he expected to grate on religious people, but, despite his elaborate approach, James never seems to *give* us a cause like this or even attempt a causal explanation at all. In fact, if you were to pick up *The Varieties* after the second or third lecture, you would be hard put to say just what he meant by the "purely existential point of view."

James's reassurances on the irrelevance of the existential judgment to the value of religion seem like a defense of his own procedure, but they turn out to be a disguised polemic against a position that bothers him as much as it would bother a traditional believer.

The attack on religion by reducing it to the effects of bodily functions (or malfunctions) James christens "medical materialism."[14] This position frightens the religious person because of the "lowly" origins assigned to religion. Yet what is there to fear? *Granted* "George Fox was an hereditary degenerate; Carlyle was undoubtedly auto-intoxicated by some organ or

---

10. Ibid., 17.
11. Ibid., 15.
12. Ibid., 17.
13. Ibid.
14. Ibid., 20.

other," but "how can such an existential account of facts of mental history decide in one way or another upon their spiritual significance?"[15]

So far this is the existential judgment as stated and defended by James. But he doesn't leave it there. Instead, he begins to attack the position he seemed to be claiming was harmless. The medical materialists fail to realize they are making two logically distinct judgments; but, more damagingly, they fail to see the inconsistency of their own position. It should follow from their view that "scientific theories are organically conditioned just as much as religious emotions are"[16] and could not be considered true "unless one have worked out in advance some psycho-physical theory connecting spiritual values in general with determinate sorts of physiological change."[17] Since such a standard has not been provided, they can't claim both that religious experience is discredited *solely because* it is organically conditioned and that their theory is *true*. This is a fairly standard objection against reductive interpretations of knowledge, but James brings up a more intriguing issue, one more reflective of what he himself will go on to do. Since he put it in a long footnote, you wonder if he was aware of all that it implied.[18]

He points out that, if we try to reinterpret religion as, say, perverted sexuality and then examine religious behavior and religious language, we find they include elements from the whole of life, all the body can offer for symbol and metaphor: "the whole organism gives overtones of comment whenever the mind is strongly stirred to expression."[19] Thus, "One might almost as well interpret religion as a perversion of the respiratory function. The Bible is full of the language of respiratory oppression."[20] If the materialist hypothesis is refined to claim *some* sort of dependence on the sex organs, it loses most of its force:

> In this sense the religious life depends just as much on the spleen, the pancreas, and the kidneys as on the sexual apparatus, and the whole theory has lost its point in evaporating into a vague general assertion of the dependence, *somehow*, of the mind upon the body.[21]

15. Ibid., 21.
16. Ibid.
17. Ibid., 22.
18. Ibid., 19–20.
19. Ibid., 19.
20. Ibid.
21. Ibid., 20.

This is a forceful and fairly complete rejection of a position James began by treating as harmless and, more pointedly, as *the sort of thing he himself was going to offer*. So the question quickly becomes: what is James going to do instead?

The revealing footnote I've been quoting from draws this conclusion:

> The plain truth is that to interpret religion one must in the end look at the immediate content of the religious consciousness. The moment one does this, one sees how wholly disconnected it is in the main from the content of the sexual consciousness. Everything about the two things differs, objects, moods, faculties concerned, and acts impelled to.[22]

From this point of view, the existential judgment as James originally describes it simply dissolves to nothing. The question of origin vanishes entirely and it becomes hard to see how the other part of the judgment, the classification of religious phenomena with "similar" phenomena of a nonreligious nature, is to be carried out at all or why it would even be attempted.

The alleged subject of James's book, religious feelings and impulses, certainly suggests a more narrow focus than the "objects, moods, faculties concerned, and acts impelled to" that make up "the immediate content of the religious consciousness." One could grant, for example, that both an Easter morning worship service and a drunken Saturday night orgy might yield feelings of joy and yet claim that what makes the one feeling religious is the total context of the experience.

Even when he goes on to argue, at several points, that there is no single feeling or impulse that is by its nature religious, he is attuned to the broader elements of the experience that make it religious or not. Here are three passages arguing three different points—the common storehouse of emotions; the defining force of "objects" of consciousness; the inadequacy (!) of psychological processes to characterize religious life—and, in each case, James is careful to note what distinguishes religious experience. Notice, too, as we get further along in the book, the increasing stress he puts on this.

First, at the beginning of Lecture II, he says that the term "religious sentiment"

> probably contains nothing whatever of a psychologically specific nature. There is religious fear, religious love, religious awe,

---

22. Ibid.

> religious joy and so forth. But religious love is only man's natural emotion of love directed to a religious object; religious fear is only the ordinary fear of commerce, so to speak, the common quaking of the human breast, in so far as the notion of divine retribution may arouse it; religious awe is the same organic thrill which we feel in a forest twilight, or in a mountain gorge; only this time it comes over us at the thought of our supernatural relations; and similarly of all the various sentiments which may be called into play in the lives of religious persons . . ..there thus seems to be no one elementary religious emotion, but only a common storehouse of emotions upon which religious objects may draw.[23]

In Lecture III, he says:

> All our attitudes, moral, practical, or emotional, as well as religious, are due to the "objects" of our consciousness, the things which we believe to exist, whether really or ideally, along with ourselves.[24]

Much later, when discussing one of the characteristics of saintliness, he refers to a work that singles out a certain psychological process—rather than a feeling—as the essence of religion; his comments are illuminating and suggest James has a clearer view of what he's doing when he finds an opposing position he wants to reject:

> On this subject I refer to the work of M. Murisier . . . who makes inner unification the mainspring of the whole religious life. But *all* strongly ideal interests, religious or irreligious, unify the mind and tend to subordinate everything to themselves. One would infer from M. Murisier's pages that this formal condition was peculiarly characteristic of religion, and that one might in comparison almost neglect material content, in studying the latter. I trust that the present work will convince the reader that religion has plenty of material content which is characteristic, and which is more important by far than any general psychological form.[25]

All of these remarks turn on the same point: the religious consciousness is distinguished by its "objects"; religion has distinctive material content and is not to be studied from the point of view of psychological processes alone. What that distinctive content is becomes a fascinating question in *The Varieties*, which the later sections of this part will consider.

23. Ibid., 33.
24. Ibid., 55.
25. Ibid., 317–18.

At this point, however, it is clear that James conceives a large part of his task to be describing the meaning of certain experiences without bringing in theology but also without reducing "the immediate content of the religious consciousness" to something else.

If we take a step back and ask how exactly this task fits into James's beginning description of this investigation, we can begin to see the source of the confusion. James really doesn't describe what in fact he will go on to do. His portrayal of religious experience is neither a search for causes nor much of a rigorous attempt to classify religious feelings with anything but themselves. But, if we turn from the existential judgment to the spiritual judgment, supposedly the judgment of "value," we can see an interesting shifting of boundaries. James had originally given three criteria for the evaluation of religious states of mind: immediate luminousness, philosophical reasonableness, and moral helpfulness.[26] Yet when he actually comes to judge saintliness, he only explicitly uses the third one, moral helpfulness. Establishing the "immediate luminousness" of these experiences and describing them in a "philosophically reasonable" way are tasks that are spread over the entire book, even the very early chapters where he claims to be taking the purely existential point of view. And these two criteria provide a good approach to searching the content of the religious consciousness. Thus, James has, in his stated aims, hidden the descriptive task within the spiritual judgment while, in practice, he has scattered this part of the inquiry all over the book.

At this point, it becomes necessary to ask: What, if anything, remains of the psychological standpoint? Also, given what he's said about the distinctiveness of religious experience, what does James hope to learn by some of the comparisons of religious experience "with other varieties of melancholy, happiness and trance"?[27] This is something he also continues throughout the book, most jarringly in the lecture on mysticism, where discussions of alcoholism, drugs and just plain "good feeling" abound.

To answer, let's start with an example from that lecture of something James thinks psychology really does contribute to a study of religion: "It seems far more likely to ascribe [the higher mystical flights] to inroads from the subconscious life, of the cerebral activity correlative to which we as yet know nothing."[28]

26. Ibid., 25.
27. Ibid., 30.
28. Ibid., 385.

What is most striking about that claim is that he doesn't make it in opposition to more theological views of mysticism but to more reductive psychological theories of mysticism, which locate its source in a degenerate brain. In other words, when James turns to the subconscious he does not mean to replace the physiological causes of the medical materialists with subconscious *causes*: he uses the subconscious to broaden our picture of experience and consciousness and to suggest how mystical experiences might be part of general human experience. He calls the idea of the subconscious life "the most important step forward that has occurred in psychology since I have been a student of that science," and thinks it "casts light on many phenomena of religious biography."[29] Thus, when James tells us he is speaking from the psychological point of view, he means at the very least that he will use the subconscious as a basic methodological tool.

It really does play a basic role in *The Varieties* and contributes to the final conclusions James feels he can draw from his study. I want to illustrate in more detail some of the things he feels the subconscious can illuminate, and this will show as well what he thinks he can learn from nonreligious comparisons. But first I have to explore further how James conceives the subconscious itself because, once again, there are ambiguities in his conception that will cause problems later.

It is possible to develop, from James's broad remarks, two different descriptions of the subconscious: one to make empiricists smile, one to make them frown.

At first, he seems to mean by it simply those interests, thoughts, and projects not presently occupying the conscious mind. Our different aims and interests are relatively independent of one another: "When one group is present and engrosses the interest, all the ideas connected with other groups may be excluded from the mental field."[30] The point here is simply that what we mean by "subconscious" is whatever is on the periphery of conscious activity and, as that activity changes, so does the periphery. In each person's consciousness, there is a part that "figures as focal and contains the excitement."[31] But it would be a mistake to conclude that one part was, is and will be the true self or that some parts are essentially "beneath" the conscious level. As our interests and tastes shift, so our centers of energy or centers of consciousness shift, and the "subconscious" is merely a name

29. Ibid., 215.
30. Ibid., 181.
31. Ibid., 182.

for those aims of ours that are not central to our present task. In fact, James explicitly rejects the term "unconscious" because of its connotations.[32]

This is a rather non-troublesome description. It makes no obvious ontological commitments—"Buddhists or Humians can perfectly well describe the facts in the phenomenal terms which are their favorites."[33] It need not imply that the content of the subconscious is anything more than what you might first pick up in experience and then ignore for a time. So far the empiricists can smile.

Elsewhere, however, James speaks of "subliminal regions of the mind,"[34] as if there were an undiscovered country beyond the horizons of the conscious life which is—in a stronger sense than that above—out there with strange things in it. It is true that he always insists that the "memories, thoughts, and feelings which are extra-marginal and outside of the primary consciousness altogether . . . must be classed as conscious facts of some sort."[35] Yet he has been credited as anticipating Jung's notion of an impersonal subconscious, and some of his statements suggest this stronger conception. For example, when discussing mysticism, he says:

> It is evident that from the point of view of their psychological mechanism, the classic mysticism and these lower mysticisms spring from the same mental level, from the great subliminal or transmarginal region of which science is beginning to admit the existence, but of which so little is really known. That region contains every kind of matter: "seraph and snake" abide there side by side.[36]

And, further on, he gives his most extensive characterization of the subliminal region (and, to clear the air of the bad smell of psychical research, he suggests we call "full sunlit consciousness" the A-region of personality):

> The B-region, then, is obviously the larger part of each of us, for it is the abode of everything that is latent and the reservoir of everything that passes unrecorded or unobserved. . . . it harbors the springs of all our obscurely motived passions, impulses, likes, dislikes, and prejudices. Our intuitions, hypotheses, fancies, superstitions, persuasions, convictions, and in general all our non-rational

32. Ibid., 193.
33. Ibid., 182.
34. Ibid., 217.
35. Ibid., 215.
36. Ibid., 384.

operations, come from it. It is the source of our dreams, and apparently they may return to it. In it arise whatever mystical experiences we may have. . . . It is also the fountain-head of much that feeds our religion. In persons deep in the religious life, . . . the door into this region seems unusually wide open.[37]

The language remains metaphorical, but James is clearly flirting with a stronger conception here. And since the subconscious will play a major role in his discussion of the truth claims of mysticism as well as in the formation of his own final conclusions, it's important to be aware of this ambiguity. The most obvious difference in the views is this: if everyone has, in varying degrees, the same sort of "subliminal region," then our dealings with this region will all be fundamentally the same; if, however, the subconscious is understood as the periphery of each person's consciousness, then it would be determined by each person's experience, and it would make no sense to speak of a "region" of consciousness that we could all be in communication with or a full-fledged "idea" that could exist in all of us independently of all religious traditions.

At this point, however, I want to stress only that the subconscious is the major conceptual item in James's existential point of view, and to note that in no sense is it a substitute for the physiological causes of the medical materialists. In the description above of the B-region, James says mystical experiences *arise in*—not that they are caused by—this region. It's no longer clear in what sense causal explanation remains as one of the purposes of the existential judgment:

> Psychology and religion are thus in perfect harmony up to this point, since both admit that there are forces seemingly outside of the conscious individual that bring redemption to his life . . . . [Psychology] diverges from Christian theology, which insists that they are direct supernatural operations of the Deity. I propose to you that we do not yet consider the divergence final, but leave the question for a while in abeyance—continued inquiry may enable us to get rid of some of the apparent discord.[38]

The subconscious will provide us with a good example of what James expects to learn from "nonreligious" subjects and experiences. As I argued above, he clearly is aware of the distinctiveness of religious experience so it is, at the very least, misleading to speak (as James continues to do) of the

37. Ibid., 433–34.
38. Ibid., 196.

"same" phenomenon appearing in insanity, alcoholism and mysticism. And yet, just as clearly, he thinks there is *some* light that can be shed by such comparisons. We can see what he means by looking at how he uses the subconscious in his analysis of conversion.

Taking his remarks on centers of energy and the periphery of consciousness as a framework, "To say that a man is 'converted' means . . . that religious ideas, previously peripheral in his consciousness, now take a central place, and that religious aims form the habitual centre of his energy."[39] The important thing to notice about these shifts of energy is that they can be very sudden and that the acquisition of ideas and formation of peripheral centers may in some persons go on almost unnoticed:

> [W]hen you get a Subject in whom the subconscious life . . . is largely developed, and in whom motives habitually ripen in silence, you get a case of which you can never give a full account, and in which, both to the Subject and the onlookers, there may appear an element of marvel.[40]

Examples of surprising shifts of energy which are most accessible to working psychologists are, of course, usually of a nonreligious sort, "consisting of unusually suggestible hypnotic subjects, and of hysteric patients."[41] Here we have, bluntly, the very thing that can be so worrying about James's approach, and we are now in a position to say in what sense it is true that the "same" phenomenon is involved here. James expects these examples to throw light on certain *formal* characteristics of the experience of a sudden shift of energy-center. Without claiming that these help us grasp the distinctive nature of religious conversions, we can still use them to highlight the formal process involved so that we do not look upon them "as if they were outside of nature's order altogether."[42] From our knowledge of these other subjects, we can draw certain conclusions:

> The most important consequence of having a strongly developed ultra-marginal life of this sort is that one's ordinary fields of consciousness are liable to incursions from it of which the subject does not guess the source, and which, therefore, take for him the form of unaccountable impulses to act, or inhibitions of action, of obsessive ideas, or even of hallucinations of sight or

39. Ibid., 183.
40. Ibid., 184–85.
41. Ibid., 216.
42. Ibid., 30.

> hearing. . . . Interpreting the unknown after the analogy of the known, it seems to me that hereafter, wherever we meet with a phenomenon of automatism . . . we are bound first of all to make search whether it be not an explosion, into the fields of ordinary consciousness, of ideas elaborated outside of those fields in subliminal regions of the mind. We should look, therefore, for its source in the Subject's subconscious life.[43]

In other words, the subconscious and the nonreligious experiences provide us with analogies by which we can interpret the formal process of conversion. And the value of these analogies appears when we consider claims based on the *process* of conversion itself: its suddenness, its violence, etc. In religious traditions strongly oriented toward something like the revival experience, there is at least a great temptation to make such claims.

One claim might be that the suddenness of conversion gives evidence of miraculous intervention: "Is an instantaneous conversion a miracle in which God is present as he is present in no change of heart less strikingly abrupt?"[44] James's conclusion is that we are not forced, simply because of a person's sudden conversion, to postulate a miraculous work of God any more than we would be in more gradual cases: "gradual" converts need not lament their mundane sanctification, for what accounts for the more spectacular cases is probably not miraculous intervention but the fact that

> in the recipient of the more instantaneous grace we have one of those subjects who are in possession of a large region in which mental work can go on subliminally, and from which invasive experiences, abruptly upsetting the equilibrium of the primary consciousness, may come.[45]

As far as miracles are concerned, both sorts of converts stand or fall together.

Another claim might be that, to enter into full membership in the community of believers, one *must* have undergone a striking experience of conversion. James insists that we look elsewhere for distinguishing marks of the Spirit:

> Were it true that a suddenly converted man as such is . . . of an entirely different kind from a natural man, . . . there surely ought to be some exquisite class-mark . . . which, so far as it went, would

43. Ibid., 216–17.
44. Ibid., 213.
45. Ibid., 219.

prove him more excellent than even the most highly gifted among mere natural men.[46]

Such a class mark is precisely what cannot be found. Again, we should rather ascribe *sudden* conversions to the possession by those involved of a "large region in which mental work can go on subliminally."

Thus, here are two possible religious claims made strictly on the basis of the striking process involved in conversion, and the introduction of psychological data allows us to cast doubt on them. But I think James has a more positive, though less explicit, purpose for his psychological comparisons, one related to the remarks I made at the beginning of this section.

I reflected earlier that James seems clearest on what he is and is not doing when he can find some other psychologist's or scientist's theory he can reject. Typically, those he rejects use the techniques and findings of psychology to discredit religious experience; dismiss it from being taken seriously, let alone admirably; to convict believers of weakness or degeneracy, linking them with the worst, most destructive, most troubled and troubling of human characters.

The difference James senses in what he is doing, without ever arguing for it, is this: when he notes the same link, he's not trying to reject religion but to uncover its human elements, to bring it into the broad human way. And he's doing the same thing, from the other direction, for the addicted and the disturbed: he brings the alcoholic as close as he can to the mystic to build a bridge, of whatever sort, between them, to see them both as part of nature's order. Both reductive psychologists and exclusive religious traditions could have similar problems with that. They live by division.

But this is the church of William James: where the sinner and the saint can lie down together, comparing their sufferings and their exaltations, sorting out the highways, detours, and dead ends of the human path.

And yet this remains very much a human connection across a human bridge. Two things need more exploration: 1/ while James grants that the distinctive nature of religion must be specified in terms of its "objects," what those amount to remains a question and will require a closer look; 2/ while James resists *reducing* religious experience to something else, he is just as resistant to *raising* religious experience to something more than it will bear, and one can wonder what this leaves him. That is, it is a basic claim of *The Varieties*, and perhaps the most questionable, that religious experience can be discussed, God and salvation can be discussed, without discussing any

46. Ibid.

of the theological and doctrinal claims of any specific religion or religious tradition.

These problems, especially the second, were the parts of *The Varieties* I struggled with the most, and what I got out of the struggle occupies the next two sections.

3. The Meaning of God in Human Experience

Through all his investigations of religious experience and his meditations on the nature of religious belief, it would be fair to say of William James that it was what was done on earth rather than in heaven that drew his attention and claimed his respect. I would say, more broadly, that it was another way of James wanting to see a thing in all its connections, to see how things fit and worked together, rather than in isolation. Still, if we recall his rough characterization of "the immediate content of the religious consciousness"—"objects, moods, faculties concerned, and acts impelled to"[47]—it would be the moods and the acts that seem peculiarly his own. James often puts so much stress on the human side of the experience that anything that might be called divine seems to vanish altogether.

But it's just that divine reality, that central thing that's encountered—not brought along—by us, that Other reality above all others, that would seem to make an experience religious and that I want to search out in this section. We can ask the question this way: What does James talk about when he talks about God? Does he talk about anything more than us?

Putting the question that way takes me back to all the debates about theories of meaning, "God talk," and the distinctiveness of religious language that loomed so large in twentieth-century Anglo-American philosophy. Looking back at James across the dismal gulf of logical positivism and its verification principle, it was tempting, and perhaps inevitable, to see James and the pragmatists as doing the same thing, though in a far less rigorous way. The "difference" and "workability" the pragmatists demanded seemed to be early versions of the verification principle; their impatience with metaphysics and theology could easily tilt toward dismissing them as nonsense. It was easy to see James flirting with the translation of religious statements into so many human gestures or declarations of subjective preference: "Hurrah!" "That feels good!" "I approve this—you do the same!" "Boo!"

47. Ibid., 20.

On Religious Life: William James and I

In a way, the logical positivists did to religious language what the medical materialists did to visions and dreams, and my guess is that James would react to the later thinkers much as he did to the earlier.

I remember spending a lot of time wrestling with these issues, both as they related to James and as general issues in the philosophy of religion; and, in the earlier stage of this writing, I spent a lot of time imagining I was sorting them out. But I now look upon this as so much wasted effort.

James was a nineteenth-century thinker. To force him into the narrow categories and fevered debates of the logical positivists is to distort him. When James says something is meaningless, he doesn't mean it's literally nonsense: he means it's pointless to argue about or doesn't make much of a difference.

It would be absurd to argue that James wanted to dismiss or dissolve religious questions: most of his books in one way or another end up grappling with just those questions. What he wanted to do, and what he saw pragmatism as helping to do, was to change the nature of those discussions. For example, he thought debating the creation of the world was meaningless, because the important issue was not its creation but its salvation.[48] (Clearly, were James to rise and visit contemporary America, he would be aghast at the debates about creationism, as well as the widespread refusal to accept evolution.) Charmingly, and typically, he later changed his mind and admitted debating creation did make a difference.[49] But in neither case would he claim the statements made in the debate were literally nonsense.

James wants to have done with debates about divine powers but *not* by simply dismissing them as senseless altogether or by reducing the meaning of religious beliefs either to emotional charges or to poetic elaborations of vital experiences. And yet, James, in his wanderings and his own poetic evocations, manages to seem as though he's arguing for positions that are quite similar to those. In fact, one of the most common impressions given by the *Pragmatism* lectures has been that, although religious beliefs may not mean anything definite, they are valuable because they grant us peace of mind in troubled times. James found this criticism frustrating and complained in his preface to *The Meaning of Truth* that

> christian and non-christian alike accuse me of summoning people to say "God exists," *even when he doesn't exist*, because forsooth in

---

48. Ibid., 528–30.
49. Ibid., 922.

my philosophy the "truth" of the saying doesn't really mean that he exists in any shape whatever, but only that to say so feels good.[50]

I think James was right to be frustrated, but the critics who so frustrated him were bearing witness, by their very distortions, to a genuine tendency of his thought. In religious experience, it's clearly what happens on the human side, apart from its wider connections, that is of the greatest importance to James, both the happening itself and its ripple effect in the lives of those involved. As I said, James's eyes are firmly on earth, not on heaven.

But his eyes were not closed to heaven or to the greater power the mystics testify to encountering, the presence-not-themselves they are struck down or lifted up by. In this section, I want to show what it is James sees on the divine side of the divine-human continuum and try to make it clear he certainly thinks, when he talks about God, that he's talking about more than us.

There is another aspect of this general problem, however, which I must discuss as well. It plays a particularly large role in *The Varieties* and has often appeared in discussions of religious belief and understanding that have nothing to do with James: seeing religion as nothing more than a way of looking at or feeling about all things. (Wittgenstein's duck-rabbit comes to mind. I'll explore this comparison more extensively in section six when I discuss James's conclusions.) This would be more than an intention to act a certain way or feel a bit more lofty than usual; it would be something like a charged global outlook.

James mentioned moods as one characteristic element of the religious consciousness. And there are passages in *The Varieties* where the mood or outlook of an individual becomes so important in his discussion that we not only lose the sense of an object of religious experience but also the sense of a definite religious *encounter*: we seem to be faced with moods that permeate the entire life of the believer—John Bunyan's melancholy, for example—which differ radically from, say, mystical experiences understood as encounters that are set apart from other events in the lives of believers. His entire discussion of healthy-mindedness would be a prime example of something that was little more than a question of mood. Still, most of the time, James preserves the sense of a divine object somewhere in the background: Bunyan was melancholy in the face of something pretty definite. And, as we'll see, even in the most extreme cases, he will still test

---

50. Ibid., 825.

religious moods by measuring them against something beyond those who have them.

This is probably the issue in *The Varieties* where James's ambiguities become most glaring, most misleading, most confusing. Part of this does come from his keeping his eyes on human things; part comes as well from the generosity and sympathy with which he enters different and opposing views. I picture him picking out the nuggets of truth he can find in each, polishing them, admiring how they look together, and declaring, "Now they're not *so* different, are they?"

But I've come to suspect there's another source of ambiguity, something at the very root of James's whole endeavor. He's looking for something beneath the warring traditions and exclusive declarations of the world's religions, a minimum that can be shared across their boundaries. But this is more than a matter of exploring religious life or contributing to religious peace. This is about human life as such. James is looking for a purity of encounter, beneath interpretation or verbal expression, something in pure experience unsullied by the particularity of creeds, yet strange and powerful and magnificent enough to be held as divine. He understands the goal of his search as the one true source of religion, and he believes, once freed of its parochial limitations, it can be a source of vitality for life on earth. I've come to suspect this quest itself is a prime source of James's ambiguity, because I decided he's trying to do something that can't be done.

But I'll take this up in the next section, when I examine more closely the sources of faith and the force of tradition. For now, let's try to see in some detail what James does talk about when he talks about God.

One of the best places to explore this (as well as, I think, one of the best places in all of James's writings to see how pragmatism works) is in Lecture XVIII, on "Philosophy," where James is considering how far philosophy and dogmatic theology are able to ground religious beliefs in certainty. James gives a brief sketch of pragmatism—with a bow to Peirce—that is a bit more "action" oriented than is usual, even for James. It's hard not to get the impression that a belief, to be significant, must make a difference to *me* and call me to *action*. James distinguishes God's metaphysical and moral attributes, and he first applies the pragmatic test to the former: they include God's necessariness, immateriality, simplicity, self-sufficiency, self-love, and a number of others.[51] The question to ask about these attributes, says James, is this:

---

51. Ibid., 400.

[H]ow do such qualities as these make any definite connection with our life? And if they severally call for no distinctive adaptation of our conduct, what vital difference can it possibly make to a man's religion whether they be true or false?[52]

This is one of the most brazen and—to James's harshest critics—most irritating formulations of pragmatism: "Who really cares? Even if what you say is true, so what? What does it *matter to me*?" And of course there is the emphasis on conduct, as opposed to thought, to complete the anti-intellectual attitude. James must have had a lot of fun doing this sort of thing, and he was so clever at it, that I can't resist quoting the polemical passage with which he crowns his attack on metaphysical theologians:

> What is their deduction of metaphysical attributes but a shuffling and matching of dictionary-adjectives, aloof from morals, aloof from human needs, something that might be worked out from the mere word "God" by one of those logical machines of wood and brass which recent ingenuity has contrived as well as by a man of flesh and blood. They have the trail of the serpent over them. One feels that in the theologians' hands, they are only a set of titles obtained by a mechanical manipulation of synonyms; verbality has stepped into the place of vision, professionalism into that of life. Instead of bread we have a stone; instead of a fish, a serpent. Did such a conglomeration of abstract terms give really the gist of our knowledge of the deity, schools of theology might indeed continue to flourish, but religion, vital religion, would have taken its flight from this world.
>
> So much for the metaphysical attributes of God! From the point of view of practical religion, the metaphysical monster which they offer to our worship is an absolutely worthless invention of the scholarly mind.[53]

The moral attributes of God, as one would expect, fare much better in James's hands. But, as one might not expect—as one might, in fact, be surprised to learn—he does not approve them solely because they clearly would affect a believer's conduct. The important thing to notice, and the thing I want to stress here, is this: James judges that the moral attributes of God, unlike the metaphysical, *imply objective connections* with the hard earth and the cold sky of the real world, and it is *because of these connections* that they are able to make a vital difference to the believer's life. It is clear

52. Ibid.
53. Ibid., 400-401.

from the way James first presents these attributes that he intends them to have much more than subjective reality.⁵⁴ Omniscience, justice, and love offer obvious connections, not only to our experience, but to the nature of the world as well. They bear on what will happen to us, not merely how we feel. So if God is omniscient, just, and loving, God can see us in the dark, judge us, and pardon us. If believing God has such qualities affects our choices, our fears, and our hopes, it does so because those qualities first assert something about what the world is like.

It might, again, be surprising to see how far James is willing to go with this line of thought. That God is *unalterable* counts as a moral attribute because it implies that "we can count on him securely."⁵⁵ Holiness and omnipotence are even clearer examples of the objective connections James has in mind: they are qualities that are not completely tied to our experience, yet James sees them as "connecting" with the world: "God's holiness, for example: being holy, God can will nothing but the good. Being omnipotent, he can secure its triumph."⁵⁶ All of these attributes have implications for our conduct but they are primarily about God's place in the world, and it is only because we understand what these attributes mean that they do have such implications. (As far as I know, the only belief that James ever granted significance to on *purely* subjective grounds was belief in the Absolute;⁵⁷ and by his next book, he had become so irritated with his critics that he took back what he said.⁵⁸)

None of these reflections, of course, do anything to establish the truth of any of those claims about God, and James is quick to wave them away, with all of speculative theology, as hopelessly inadequate to create or sustain real faith. But this passage is important for offering an unusually clear illustration of the way pragmatism is used by James, and it's an important corrective to overly subjective interpretations of his approach. Later, we'll see that the insistence on objective consequences will serve as a reason for James's adoption of what he calls "piecemeal" supernaturalism. For now, here's a nice summary of this point, taken from his concluding lecture:

> Only when . . . remote objective consequences are predicted, does religion, as it seems to me, get wholly free from the first

---

54. Ibid., 401.
55. Ibid.
56. Ibid.
57. Ibid., 519.
58 Ibid., 824–25.

> immediate subjective experience, and bring a *real hypothesis* into play.... God, meaning only what enters into the religious man's experience of union, falls short of being an hypothesis of this more useful order. He needs to enter into wider cosmic relations in order to justify the subject's absolute confidence and peace.... Religion, in her fullest exercise of function is not a mere illumination of facts already given, not a mere passion, like love, which views things in a rosier light. It is indeed that, as we have seen abundantly. But it is something more, namely, a postulator of new *facts* as well.... It must be such that different events can be expected in it, different conduct must be required.[59]

There is, moreover, something else we shouldn't overlook. Even when James turns back from the farther reaches of the universe to where his heart lies, in the human struggle, he understands religious faith as involving more than human qualities. Philosophers who have understood religious language as being about nothing more than disguised speech about human emotion, human commitment, and (perhaps higher) human ways of looking at the world would certainly find a sympathetic partner in William James and much in his writings to support their views. But, however important he feels these elements are, however necessary he thinks it is to insist on them in the face of too much theological abstraction, there is one thing more he sees in faith and it's at the very heart of *The Varieties*: a vital encounter with powers beyond the self, the surrender of self to a divine object. It's the conversion experience that becomes definitive for James in revealing the essence of religion (in the following passage, specifically Christianity):

> One may say that the whole development of Christianity in inwardness has consisted in little more than the greater and greater emphasis attached to this crisis of self-surrender. From Catholicism to Lutheranism, and then to Calvinism; from that to Wesleyanism; and from this, outside of technical Christianity altogether, to pure "liberalism" or transcendental idealism, whether or not of the mind-cure type, taking in the medieval mystics, the quietists, the pietists, and quakers by the way, we can trace the stages of progress towards the idea of an immediate spiritual help, experienced by the individual in his forlornness and standing in no essential need of doctrinal apparatus or propitiatory machinery.[60]

---

59. Ibid., 462–63.
60. Ibid., 196.

On Religious Life: William James and I

James, crucially, takes both mysticism and prayer seriously, encounters and appeals to something beyond the self, meetings in which real transactions take place, where power is restored and aid given. This should destroy the widespread impression that James is interested only in action, that religious beliefs for him are at best motivational slogans, at worst tranquilizers. And it should distinguish him from those philosophers who would translate or reduce religious faith exclusively to human terms. James has both a richer view of the possibilities of experience and a greater willingness to take a religious picture of the universe seriously.

He thinks he can at least establish that the boundaries of human experience are broader than we might normally think and that they open some space where religious encounters might take place:

> It is as if there were in the human consciousness a *sense of reality, a feeling* of *objective presence, a perception* of what we may call "*something there*," more deep and more general than any of the special and particular "senses" by which the current psychology supposes existent realities to be originally revealed.[61]

Just as the notion of a "shift of mental energy" helped us understand the process of conversion, so the isolating of such a perception establishes the possibility, the profane structure, of the specifically religious encounter:

> We may now lay it down as certain that in the distinctively religious sphere of experience, many persons (how many we cannot tell) possess the objects of their beliefs, not in the form of mere conceptions which their intellect accepts as true, but rather in the form of quasi-sensible realities directly apprehended. As his sense of the real presence fluctuates, so the believer alternates between warmth and coldness in his faith.[62]

And he uses a charming image to suggest how a believer's entire life might be animated by such perceptions:

> They determine our vital attitudes as decisively as the vital attitude of lovers is determined by the habitual sense, by which each is haunted, of the other being in the world.[63]

The further question in *The Varieties*, once we grasp the importance of encountering some divine reality, becomes how exactly to describe that

61. Ibid., 59.
62. Ibid., 64.
63. Ibid., 72.

reality. At the end of the above quotation on the essence of religion, it's noteworthy that James stresses that the experiences he is speaking of stand "in no essential need of doctrinal apparatus." I think he tends to see, not all of religious language, but the official creeds and explicit theologies of the world's faiths as so much poetry; he would understand part of his task as reformulating these poetic statements, especially when they are used to describe experience, into statements of a philosophically reasonable sort, producing a kind of ideal-type for the philosopher of religion to work on. Here is where I began to have my greatest problem with *The Varieties*, and the following section will display my struggle with it. But the more directly we face this problem the more James's ambiguities begin to blur things.

Interestingly enough, James begins his third lecture—"The Reality of the Unseen"—by discussing not *realities* beyond the self but the power that *beliefs* and *ideals* can exert over us. He describes beliefs held so intensely they make us feel "presences that we are impotent articulately to describe."[64] He doesn't bother to distinguish between an intensely felt idea and a felt presence (which may or may not be describable). There is clearly a difference, and in the next section I'll explore the nature of that difference and what effects neglecting it has for James's investigation.

(This neglect really throws a cloud over his concept of religious experience; it creates problems that James never dealt with but which hang over this vital issue of the relation of belief to experience. Does a "felt presence" constitute in itself a religious object? Is it amenable to many interpretations? In what sense can we say the *experience itself* guides us or forms the foundation of our religion if we can't even describe it? In fact, if we want to talk about intensely felt *ideas*, then it looks as though theology should be given credit for forming experience instead of vice versa.)

For now, I'd like to round out this discussion by looking more closely at some of the passages in *The Varieties* where James really does seem to allow religious objects (or any sense of an actual encounter) to be swallowed up by religious *moods*.

As I noted at the beginning of this section, some of this comes from James's reluctance to make his definitions too exclusive. He sees no reason to suppose that there is only one distinctive object of religious experience.[65] He also is happy to gather "godless or quasi-godless creeds" like Buddhism and "Emersonianism" within the sphere of religion because they resemble

64. Ibid., 57.
65. Ibid., 33.

more deity-centered religions in the appeal they make to individuals and the kind of responses they call forth.[66]

As I have argued, James conceives of the appeals and responses of the religious life very broadly. Here we see him broadening the scope of divinity to include "any object that is god*like,* whether it be a concrete deity or not."[67] Here is a summary statement in which we can watch the ambiguities sliding as we read:

> Whatever then were most primal and enveloping and deeply true might at this rate be treated as godlike, and a man's religion might thus be identified with his attitude, whatever it might be, towards what he felt to be the primal truth.[68]

Then, in the very next paragraph, he says, "Religion, whatever it is, is a man's total reaction upon life."[69] We shift from whatever is most primal, enveloping, and true to whatever anyone's total reaction to life is. James immediately wonders why we shouldn't simply define religion—presumably without divinities—as *any* "total reaction upon life"; he's clearly tempted to do this, but allows that it would be "inconvenient, however defensible it might remain on logical grounds."[70]

This is a bit glib and, as I have been at pains to show, says far too little of what James himself is committed to: that at the heart of the religious life there is an encounter with greater powers, realities beyond the attitudes and reactions of the self. Furthermore, whenever James feels the temptation to see in religion nothing but an outlook, a mood, or "total reaction," he draws back by measuring our outlooks and reactions against the hard realities of life.

When faced, for example, with the clever cynicism of Voltaire, James could easily have pointed out the utter *lack* of anything that could be called a "religious object" in order to disqualify such a way of life as "religious." What he does, however, is try to show there is something *inadequate in the attitude itself.* His final characterization of the "godlike," then, is as follows (and here we can watch the ambiguities slide in the other direction, from "attitude" to "experience" to "primal reality"):

66. Ibid., 38.
67. Ibid.
68. Ibid., 39.
69. Ibid.
70. Ibid., 40.

> There must be something solemn, serious, and tender about any attitude which we denominate religious. If glad, it must not snicker or grin; if sad, it must not scream or curse. It is precisely as being *solemn* experiences that I wish to interest you in religious experiences. So I propose . . . to narrow our definition once more by saying that the word "divine," as employed therein, shall mean for us not merely the primal and enveloping and real, for that meaning if taken without restriction might well be too broad. The divine shall mean for us only such a primal reality as the individual feels impelled to respond to solemnly and gravely, and neither by a curse nor a jest.[71]

We might say that the distinction between the healthy-minded and the sick soul, which I'll discuss presently, is nothing more than the isolation of the "glad" and "sad" poles of this definition.

But first I want to shade this picture a bit more. After James defines the boundaries of religion, he wants to show there are elements in religion that are not contained in morality, and he uses Marcus Aurelius as an example of morality. Here's another fascinating display of ambiguities where James notes what is clearly a difference in divine object, between the stoic *anima mundi* and the Christian God, yet *presents* the difference as one of *emotional atmosphere*:

> The *anima mundi*, to whose disposal of his personal destiny the Stoic consents is there to be respected and submitted to, but the Christian God is there to be loved; and the difference of emotional atmosphere is like that between an arctic climate and the tropics, though the outcome in the way of accepting actual conditions uncomplainingly may seem in abstract terms to be much the same.[72]

A bit later in this same discussion, James breaks into one of his songs of praise for this difference of atmosphere which I find too charming not to include:

> If religion is to mean anything definite for us, it seems to me that we ought to take it as meaning this added dimension of emotion, this enthusiastic temper of espousal, in regions where morality strictly so called can at best but bow its head and acquiesce. It ought to mean nothing short of this new reach of freedom for us,

---

71. Ibid., 42.
72. Ibid., 45.

with the struggle over, the keynote of the universe sounding in our ears, and everlasting possession spread before our eyes.[73]

As this passage clearly shows, James at times is happy to think of religion solely as an "added dimension of emotion." What I want to insist on, and what I think is displayed clearly in his contrast of stoics and Christians, is that within such dimensions of emotion, there is implied something about life and the world beyond the self, something about the way things are both in the vast universe and in the vital parts of our experience (for example, sickness and death, to choose two nonsubjective realities) that helps determine this added dimension of emotion, this new reach of freedom.

Thus, James's major division of religious types, the healthy-minded and the sick soul, would seem to be cut along the lines of temperament; yet there are distinctive beliefs involved in each, both about the universe as a whole and the significance of various parts of our mortal life.

Of the two types, healthy-mindedness is the less metaphysical: it can easily become no more than a resolution to "feel good" most of the time. It provides James with examples of religious individuals whose only belief is a will-to-be-happy. And yet, in defense of this attitude, "we must ... acknowledge," he says, "that the more complex ways of experiencing religion are new manners of producing happiness."[74] Thus, he thinks healthy-mindedness has strong affinities with traditional religions; beyond that, "healthy-mindedness as a religious attitude is ... consonant with important currents in human nature"[75] and is a "psychic type to be studied with respect."[76] Healthy-minded individuals are those "in whom religious gladness, being in possession from the outset, needs no deliverance from any antecedent burden."[77] Happiness is in our grasp: we have only to turn our minds to it.

This is probably the most blatant example of an attitude qualifying as a religion; and James is aware of the lack of theology in the mind-cure movement. But what grates most on him is the refusal of the mind-curers to come up with a proposed view of the universe in which evil is given a

---

73. Ibid., 50.
74. Ibid., 77.
75. Ibid., 88.
76. Ibid., 93.
77. Ibid., 79.

realistic place.⁷⁸ And yet he manages to find in it *some* implications about the nature of the universe above and beyond the steady beating of happy hearts:

> The fundamental pillar on which it rests is nothing more than the general basis of all religious experience, the fact that man has a dual nature, and is connected with two spheres of thought, a shallower and a profounder sphere, in either of which he may learn to live more habitually.⁷⁹

And here is a clear indication that James understands the will-to-be-happy as *some* sort of encounter with at least a god*like* object: "It is but giving your little private convulsive self a rest, and finding that a greater Self is there."⁸⁰

But, once again, it is the inadequacy of the attitude itself that is crucial. The primary theoretical difference between healthy-mindedness and morbid-mindedness is the *significance* accorded to evil and suffering. While healthy-mindedness advises us to minimize the place we give pain and the thought of pain in our lives, more pessimistic religions take such advice as not only unrealistic but superficial: the religion of a sick soul maximizes evil, so to speak, holding that the "evil aspects of life are of its very essence" and must be faced squarely if we are to grasp life's meaning.⁸¹ Sickness, death, wounds physical and spiritual, betrayal, war, pestilence, famine—these things happen and can't be thought away. There *is* no bright side of things on this earth. Healthy-mindedness enjoins us to *isolate* our moments of happiness and try to prolong them; for the sick soul, the presence of evil is palpable; nothing can be isolated from it. Here the difference ceases to be merely theoretical:

> Not the conception or intellectual perception of evil, but the grisly blood-freezing heart-palsying sensation of it close upon one, and no other conception or sensation able to live for a moment in its presence.⁸²

There is simply too much suffering built into life for us to ignore it: not morbid thoughts born of melancholy minds, but painful *events*, disease,

---

78. Ibid., 102–3.
79. Ibid., 93.
80. Ibid., 106.
81. Ibid., 124.
82. Ibid., 151.

death. Moreover, the presence of these things shadows the few moments of happiness granted our thirsting souls:

> Let sanguine healthy-mindedness do its best with its strange power of living in the moment and ignoring and forgetting, still the evil background is really there to be thought of, and the skull will grin in at the banquet.[83]

While he takes healthy-mindedness much more seriously than, say, Voltaire's cynicism considered as a worldview, he still judges it by its failure to engage clear realities:

> [M]orbid-mindedness ranges over the wider scale of experience.... evil facts ... are a genuine portion of reality; and they may after all be the best key to life's significance, and possibly the only openers of our eyes to the deepest levels of truth.[84]

Since a religion is a "total reaction upon life," if such a reaction were a narrow one, if our beliefs broke down in the face of bitter experience (like the death of a loved one or the betrayal of a friend), then those beliefs—to use a favorite (and vague) expression of James—would not get us into satisfactory relations with our experience. Healthy-mindedness is inadequate because there are certain basic things about our lives it ignores. And, as he says in the above passage, it's our encounters with just those things that can reveal to us what is most real. Thus, though this seems like a quarrel between temperaments, it's what lies beyond the self, some touching of a primal reality, that remains crucial.

Moreover, in the experience of the sick soul, we have what is for James the prime example of the difference divinity makes in the world here and now: conversion, healing, deliverance. The sick soul, suffering in the face of evil, is delivered from melancholy or from the oppression of sin by the grace of God. The conversion here, as we might expect, is not, like Newman's, from one sect to another but from one emotional state to another, almost from one life to another, from despair to happiness.

Conversion might still be taken as only a shift of temperament, but it is a shift carried out within a certain view of the universe, however bare that view may be: where evil and suffering are considered basic elements of reality, where there is another realm to which we can appeal for aid and which can affect our deliverance, where an encounter with some godlike object

---

83. Ibid., 132.
84. Ibid., 152.

is decisive. However important religious moods and temperaments are for James, however much he seems to speak only about us when he speaks about God, it is still the encounter with the divine that is essential. Here is a passage sorting this out from late in the book, when he is summing up the value of saintliness:

> Single attributes of saintliness may, it is true, be temperamental endowments, found in non-religious individuals. But the whole group of them forms a combination which, as such, is religious, for it seems to flow from the sense of the divine as from its psychological centre.[85]

But, as I remarked above, the important question in *The Varieties* is the one that arises when this discussion ends: What exactly does James think we sense in the encounter with the divine and how far can that, by itself, create and sustain the religious life? Answering that question uncovers the deepest assumptions of *The Varieties*, and those became my greatest problem with it.

One of the most valuable parts for me, in studying *The Varieties*, and what gave James such force as a philosopher of religion, was how, with the testimonies he gathered, he stretched the boundaries of *human* experience. But, oddly, at the same time, he seemed to narrow the boundaries of *religious* experience, its sources of vitality, strength, and vision. In a way, the problem I dealt with in this section would return in a different, and more troublesome, form.

4. Tradition and the Individual Believer

I heard a lecture, when I was serving as a pastor, which I only recall for a single observation; but it was one of those remarks that seem simple, obvious, and, at the same time, revelatory. I can't remember the subject of the lecture, where or when I heard it, or who delivered it. It might have been something about "the church in a changing world," something Christians have been lecturing on for going on two thousand years. The speaker could have been Stanley Hauerwas because the observation I remember seems like the sort of thing he would say.

At any rate, the speaker was discussing, or had been asked about, dialogues with non-Christians and nonbelievers, and here's the remark I

---

85. Ibid., 334.

remember: "Well, if people ask me what the Christian faith is about, or what we believe, the last thing I'd do is hand them a copy of the Apostles' Creed. Or the Bible. I'd invite them to come to worship with me and pray and sing with us."

Simple, obvious, and a pointed reorientation of what religious dialogue should be and how to begin it. It was also an implicit critique of the way we usually face the world, with our ideas and moral declarations, as though our stories, our gestures of beauty, and our life together were not our real treasures.

I've quoted that observation a lot over the years. I think it's one of those things we know but keep forgetting. We're only repeating Jesus' first explanation of himself to his disciples: "Come and see. Come with me." It reminds us that our strength and our way is not in what we think about the world, but how we live in it.

In the congregation I'm now a member of, I could show an inquirer the homeless shelter we support, the food pantry we help staff, the garden we plant so the pantry can offer fresh vegetables, the quilts we send all over the world. I'd tell about the series of talks we hosted to understand Islam. But, yes, above all, I would show the thing that sustains all these generous activities: the worship gathering of ordinary people, as nasty and narrow-minded as anyone else, but called constantly to a different life. (I still find it fascinating, and a startling truth about religious people, that they *sing together* so much about this new life.) I would want especially to show my guest the worship cycle of Holy Week, from the procession with palms, through the supper and the foot-washing and the stripping of the altar, to the adoration of the cross, ending with the candlelight service of the Easter Vigil, with its long cycle of readings, its baptisms, and its celebration of the Eucharist in the light of the resurrection. I would hope to give some sense of the story we tell about the world, the story we live in.

Here's my point: the more clearly I wanted to demonstrate what the Christian faith as I understand, live, and share it was about, where its strength and force came from, the more (not the less) particular, idiosyncratic, and detailed I would have to get, and the more people I would have to involve. That is, I would find myself bringing in the very things James wants to set aside.

He would, of course, agree that the ideas and dogmas religious people arrive at are only pale reflections of a vibrant religious life, the poorest of avenues into the truth and power of faith, but, as *The Varieties* testifies,

James chooses to show something else entirely for that purpose: the experiences of fascinating people at the very edge of life, people who have escaped the chains of tradition and the comfort of companions to confront ultimate things in their purity.

It struck me that James was a bit like a charismatic pastor, come to a town of tired old churches, proud of being so beyond the old denominations and divisions that he won't admit any real difference between a Methodist and a Sufi. He comes to gather his sheep from everyone else's flock, snatching the most vibrant and energetic, the most disturbed and driven, out of their polite prisons, washing them clean of the impurities of compromise and the distortions of imitators, dilettantes, and pedants. He would gather them into a community of solitaries, but he would make of them a Holy Remnant, the true church.

When I began studying *The Varieties*, I wanted very much to believe that something like that made sense. I shared that loose assumption about the power and primacy of individual experience, and I really did want to escape the chains of tradition and the oppressive comfort of companions. I liked, and I still treasure, the openness of James's vision, how he was as quick to embrace the different and the strange as others were to fear and reject them. I thought his shaping of the nature of religion was a way of freeing the power of that openness and establishing its enduring presence in human life.

But this became the very point at which James and I parted company, as well as a turning point in my own understanding of religious life. Wrestling with, and trying to defend, what James assumed about religious life set me on the path to the understanding of faith I sketched at the beginning of this section. Deciding how and why James was wrong made it possible for me to enter a life within that understanding.

As is true of so much that shapes *The Varieties*, the assumptions about religious life that provide the foundation for James's approach are nowhere set out and argued for explicitly. But they are implicit in that approach, and it's not hard to draw them from his words.

It seemed to me that the position taken by James on the nature and truth of religious life rested on three assumptions of increasing strength: 1/ that there is a kind of experience that transcends creeds, showing up in the lives of people who profess different faiths, and yet being essentially the same sort of experience, differing only in the interpretations placed upon it; 2/ that it makes sense to speak of this experience, even without the interpretive categories of the various faith traditions, as "religious" experience—i.e., that the experience, all by itself, is of religious significance; and 3/ that such experiences form the foundation of all religious life.

Restate these assumptions as questions and you have the problems they gave me:

1. *Is* there a common experience that shows up in different religious contexts but that is essentially the same, differing only in the various interpretations placed on it?

2. Supposing there is, i.e., granting that essentially the same experience shows up within different religious contexts, is the experience *all by itself*, before any interpretation or description by religious concepts, something we would call "religious"? (I think it's of note that this second problem can be given both a sacred and profane formulation. A theologian might claim it makes little sense to speak of religion apart from all explicit faith statements. An atheist might insist we're dealing with strange experiences that are only considered religious because religious interpretations are forced upon them. Both would agree that the experience itself, however strange, uncanny, disturbing, or overwhelming it might be, only gains whatever significance it has from theological categories or professions of faith, which must be accepted or rejected on other grounds.)

3. Finally, even granting the first two assumptions, can we further claim that these experiences are the foundation of all religious life—ritual, theology, congregational formation, codes of conduct, visions of aspiration, etc.?

Let's take them in order.

1/ Experience

Curiously enough, the title of James's book—*Varieties*—would seem to imply he would reject any claim that there was a single type of religious experience, and his own position *is* more complex than a simple claim of that sort would be. Yet James is constantly claiming that the experiences he deals with are "essentially" the same. This is a claim that is often heard about mysticism; but, for James, mysticism is the "root and centre" of "personal religious experience."[86] So, if James is making such a claim,

---

86. Ibid., 342.

he's making it not only about mysticism but about religious experience in general. He's also making it without much of an attempt to establish such a uniformity. To my knowledge, the single example of James actually comparing two experiences to establish their similarity is in his chapter on healthy-mindedness; he compares a passage from a mind-cure writer to a passage from a Catholic writer discussing contemplation. Wherein, he asks, does the description given in the mind-cure passage "*intrinsically* differ from the practice of 'recollection' which plays so great a part in Catholic discipline?"[87] He answers by saying that of course "the external associations of the Catholic discipline" differ from the other but that "the purely spiritual part of the exercise is identical in both communions."[88] That's the extent of the comparison. The Catholic writer speaks of "God," the mind-cure writer of "the spirit of continual prayer"; James sees no reason to sort out what is and what is not an "external association." We will return to this issue, but the point I'm illustrating here is that James seems to assume from the beginning that the important part, "the purely spiritual part," of the two experiences is *identical*.

So how strongly are we to take "identical"? James sits loosely on his generalizations and he was always happy to use whatever exaggeration would serve his current purposes. Also, he scorned a kind of reasoning that he saw in his philosophical contemporaries that he termed "vicious intellectualism": the assumption that sharp, exclusive distinctions in conceptual systems reflected (or dictated) sharp, exclusive distinctions in reality. (In religious studies, on this issue, James would have the extravagant language of mystical writers, careless of the limits of orthodoxy, on his side.) I think it would be fair to say that James saw the experiences that interested him as fairly uniform, while allowing that each had its own peculiarities. As we'll see, this is another crucial issue in *The Varieties* where James is comfortable with ambiguity, finding enough unity to keep the variety from shutting him out and enough variety to keep the unity from oppressing him.

(I remarked above that, when I began to study *The Varieties* seriously, I wanted to believe that something like James's approach to the religious life made the most sense of any. I was hardly alone in this. Looking back, I can effortlessly imagine my contemporaries airily proclaiming both sides of this issue with no thought of contradiction: "of course, there are all different sorts of religious experiences!" and "of course, they're all basically

---

87. Ibid., 110.
88. Ibid., 111.

alike!" Many paths, One Way, I suppose. I think now that what united this superficial ecumenism was an anti-authoritarian stance that resisted the dogmatic threats, and embraced the tolerant offerings, of both variety and unity. I would say this was fairly similar to the impulse James was following in his explorations.)

But now let's take a closer look at what exactly the experience James is pursuing looks like. In his lecture on mysticism and, later, in his concluding lecture, he lists the common characteristics of first mysticism and then the religious life in general. Examining these passages should help us focus a bit more clearly on what James wants to claim about the universal character of the basic religious experience. Here's what he gives as the "four marks" of mysticism: 1. ineffability, 2/ noetic quality, 3/ transiency, 4/ passivity. (The latter two, says James, "are less sharply marked but are usually found."[89]) He sets them out at the beginning of his discussion of mysticism, not as the result of an empirical investigation, but as a plausible enough grouping "for the purpose of the present lectures."[90] They're not intended to summarize the universal traits of mysticism but to suggest a set of boundaries for the discussion that is to follow: "These four characteristics are sufficient to mark out a group of states of consciousness peculiar enough to deserve a special name and to call for careful study."[91]

At the end of the lecture, he qualifies his presentation of a "common core" of mysticism again:

> But even this presumption from the unanimity of mystics is far from being strong. In characterizing mystic states as pantheistic, optimistic, etc., I am afraid I over-simplified the truth. I did so for expository reasons, and to keep the closer to the classic mystical tradition. The classic religious mysticism, it now must be confessed, is only a "privileged case." It is an *extract*, kept true to type by the selection of the fittest specimens and their preservation in "schools." It is carved out from a much larger mass; and if we take the larger mass as seriously as religious mysticism has historically taken itself, we find that the supposed unanimity largely disappears. . . . The fact is that the mystical feeling of enlargement, union, and emancipation has no specific intellectual content whatever of its own. It is capable of forming matrimonial alliances with material furnished by the most diverse philosophies

---

89. Ibid., 342–43.
90. Ibid., 342.
91. Ibid., 344.

and theologies, provided only they can find a place in their framework for its peculiar emotional mood. We have no right, therefore, to invoke its prestige as distinctively in favor of any special belief.[92]

This is a revealing and important quotation, for two reasons. First, it is a clear rejection of the "unanimity" of mystics *as a basis* for serious theological or philosophical claims. Coming at the end of his discussion of mysticism, this seems to underline that his list of mystical characteristics was meant only as a methodological tool. But note the antiauthoritarian language (and sense the protectiveness) in the last sentence: no *right* exists to use the *prestige* of mysticism in favor of some *special* belief. As he goes on to mention his nemesis, absolute idealism, as one of those special beliefs, it's clear he's trying to free an experience he considers significant by itself from any intellectual system that would exploit it. This is a good illustration of one way James handles the "universal" character of religious experience: he is happy to offer a list of essential qualities and claim that diverse religious experiences are alike "in all essential respects," when he wants to display a kind of experience he values and treasures; but he draws back from claiming the similarity is striking enough to use as a foundation for theoretical claims when he senses there's a danger the experience might be exploited, distorted, or limited for some alien purpose.

The second reason I find this passage revealing is that I think it's quite possible, through the first half, to take James to mean that the *experiences themselves* offer us—as he said at the beginning of the lecture—"all sorts of gradations and mixtures."[93] But, by the end, he's primarily concerned with denying a "specific intellectual content" to mystical feeling, explicitly mentioning only differences in philosophies and theologies. It sounds like the only real variety is in the interpretations and that there still could be a fairly uniform experience involved in all cases. (The ambiguity here is like the slipperiness discussed in the last section between primal realities and total reactions.) It's simply not clear at all times what James wants to call an experience and what he wants to call an interpretation.

We'll return to this problem shortly, when we try to decide what for James is and is not an "over-belief," his term for a belief that goes beyond what is contained in a religious experience. For now, let's look at the second list I mentioned above, his summary of the characteristics of the religious life in general, which opens his final lecture.

92. Ibid., 383–84.
93. Ibid., 344.

At first sight, this summary seems to be offered as more than a rough grouping for a limited purpose. It stands at the end of the entire inquiry, draped in the mantle of empiricism: "the characteristics of the religious life, as we have found them."[94]

For purposes of comparison, let's call this List A:

1. That the visible world is part of a more spiritual universe from which it draws its chief significance;

2. That union or harmonious relation with that higher universe is our true end;

3. That prayer or inner communion with the spirit thereof—be that spirit "God" or "law"—is a process wherein work is really done, and spiritual energy flows in and produces effects, psychological or material, within the phenomenal world.

Religion also includes the following psychological characteristics:

4. A new zest which adds itself like a gift to life, and takes the form either of lyrical enchantment or of appeal to earnestness and heroism.

5. An assurance of safety and a temper of peace, and, in relation to others, a preponderance of loving affections.[95]

(A bit later in the same lecture, James gives another statement of the "common nucleus" of the religious life.[96] I remember finding this second formulation, when I came upon it, as a little too much like a conceptual ambush, stated in such terms as to leave the reader's mind open for the Jamesian subconscious to stroll comfortably in. I want to discuss this when I evaluate James's theoretical conclusions. For now, I'll note he makes an equally strong claim for this second summary, presenting it as an empirical conclusion: "The warring gods and formulas of the various religions do indeed cancel each other, but there is a certain uniform deliverance in which religions all appear to meet.[97])

Although he makes an apparently strong, empirical claim for these concluding summaries, there are two serious qualifications that must be made about that claim.

---

94. Ibid., 435.
95. Ibid.
96. Ibid., 454.
97. Ibid.

In the first place, List A is quite similar to the "composite photograph of universal saintliness" given in lectures XI, XII, and XIII.[98] This earlier list of saintly characteristics bears the same relation to its discussion as the four mystical marks bore to theirs: it comes relatively close to the beginning of the discussion and it seems to function as a framing or organizing principle for the remarks that follow. Lets call this List B:

1. A feeling of being in a wider life than that of this world's selfish little interests; and a conviction, not merely intellectual, but as it were sensible, of the existence of an Ideal Power ...

2. A sense of the friendly continuity of the ideal power with our own life, and a willing self-surrender to its control.

3. An immense elation and freedom, as the outlines of the confining selfhood melt down.

4. A shifting of the emotional centre towards loving and harmonious affections, toward "yes, yes," and away from "no," where the claims of the non-ego are concerned.[99]

If we compare Lists A and B, we can see they differ primarily in phrasing and minor details: List B is phrased more from the viewpoint of the individual, while points 1–3 of List A, as befits a set of conclusions, assume a more cosmic point of view, omitting talk of "feelings" and "senses." Still, points 1–3 of List A are close enough to 1–2 of List B, and 4–5 of List A to 3–4 of List B to make us doubt that List A is the set of empirically determined conclusions James presents it as. It seems most likely both lists are alternate descriptions of something James began, not ended, with. He came to the witnesses of the religious life looking for a way of feeling and living and seeing the world that called to him deeply. He wanted to say he discovered it there; I think it would be too much to say he created it there, but I decided finally that he didn't discover enough for what he wanted to do. How much or how little there is of a common religious experience remains unclear and too weakly supported by the witnesses. If anything, although it's the establishing of some sort of pre-creedal unity that he needs (and often claims), the witnesses don't tilt toward unity but toward variety.

This brings me to the second serious qualification, and I found it in James's own words, later in his concluding lecture:

---

98. Ibid., 249.
99. Ibid., 249–50

> I am expressly trying to reduce religion to its lowest admissible terms, to that minimum, free from individualistic excrescences, which all religions contain as their nucleus, and on which it may be hoped that all religious persons may agree. That established, we should have a result which might be small, but would at least be solid; and on it and round it the ruddier additional beliefs on which the different individuals make their venture might be grafted, and flourish as richly as you please. I shall add my own over-belief . . . , and you will, I hope, also add your over-beliefs, and we shall soon be in the varied world of concrete religious constructions once more.[100]

Once again, there is the blithe claim of universality: "all religious persons" can agree on a nucleus "all religions" contain. Once again, there is the polemical language against traditions that might claim too exclusive an ownership: they are "individualistic excrescences" which must be "grafted" on the nucleus. But note and ponder the phrase "concrete religious constructions" in the last line of the passage. This surprised me when I first came across it because it seemed to imply a reversal of goals: if it's the over-beliefs, the excrescences grafted back onto the nucleus, that make religion *concrete* after all, then they seem to have an importance James has spent a long set of lectures denying. This is the issue we'll turn to now.

It's clear that James doesn't want the jolting, expansive, awe-inspiring experiences he values trapped within the particular and exclusive boundaries of any of the world's recognized religions. The question is: How much of those religions, with their explicit claims and characteristic practices, can he eliminate and still claim he has something of *religious* significance? Perhaps we might put it more pointedly: Does James himself have a right to invoke the prestige of religion for the little he's willing to accept?

2/ Interpretation and Significance

As I noted above, this is a problem that can be raised by believer and nonbeliever alike. Both could admit that James has gathered an impressive collection of tales, showing what we are capable of running into at the extremes of our nature and experience. But the believer would insist, for the experience to be religious, it must be informed (when it is not already shaped) by definite beliefs which will then give it content, value, direction;

---

100. Ibid., 450–51.

the nonbeliever could, in a sense, insist the same, arguing that nothing in any experience demanded to be seen as religious and that no experience, however abnormal, could force us to take it that way without some interpretation provided after the fact. It's probably only fair to say that James would undoubtedly enjoy falling somewhere between such antagonists.

Let's begin by considering some overlapping descriptions.

Suppose I'm describing something strange that happened to me, a night vision so exciting and beyond the normal that I keep rephrasing my description and developing my story. If you were taking notes and setting down my descriptions in a series, you might end up with something like this:

1. I saw a strange light in my room and felt that I was not alone. I also felt my body undergoing some mysterious change.
2. I saw a strange light in my room and felt a presence so wonderful that I never wanted to be parted from it.
3. A strange light and an invisible presence filled my room with glory and transformed my soul last night. I shall never be the same.
4. I encountered God last night. I seemed to myself to disappear in that glory.
5. I had a vision of God the Father last night. Without words or actions, he washed me clean and reshaped my soul.
6. Last night, I was transformed into Dante Alighieri and saw three colored circles with one circumference, which image was in fact the Holy Trinity, much as the Council of Nicaea had defined it, spinning within a light in my room.

Call this an interpretation scale. Reading down the list, where would we say we're leaving description and moving into interpretation? #6 is filled with explicit content which seems obviously imported into whatever went on (though we'll see later that things may not be so simple). Most people would sense the presence of a Christian interpreter in #5 with the naming of God as "the Father" and the baptismal reference to washing clean in describing whatever happened. #1 would probably bother no one who hasn't read much about the involvement of language in perception. #2, #3, and #4 might all be debatable, though reference to "God" and "glory" might suggest some interpretive nudging in #4.

Now, once we move up the scale and reach a level beyond which we feel obliged to speak of interpretation, of religious beliefs and faith statements being brought into the description, the question becomes: Are the statements *below* that level, without further elaboration, of religious significance? Most people would probably consider #1 to be of not much significance at all, or anything more than curious. #2 and #3 would be the most fruitfully debatable and the most likely to be seen as somehow needing to be taken in some religious sense. I would guess James might be comfortable with #2 through #5, in his easy way, though #2 and #3 seem to offer what he most needs.

For an issue I see as so basic to *The Varieties*, James doesn't spend much time discussing interpretation and experience or even describing in much detail what he understands by experience. I thought it would be helpful to approach this issue by using the distinction I mentioned in the last section between a sense of "presence," of "something there," and an *idea* which is apprehended almost sensibly. This will offer a neat pair of bookends for my interpretation scale. Then we should see what the subconscious might offer on this point.

Here is an example James cites of an experience of a "felt presence":

> "There was not a mere consciousness of something there, but fused in the central happiness of it, a startling awareness of some ineffable good. Not vague either, not like the emotional effect of some poem, or scene, or blossom, or music, but the sure knowledge of the close presence of a sort of mighty person, and after it went, the memory persisted as the one perception of reality. Everything else might be a dream, but not that."[101]

This seems a clear case of an experience, fairly striking in itself, which could be taken as relatively free of interpretation, just the sort of case James has in mind.

Now consider a vividly felt *idea*. Here the experience could be, say, a vision *of Christ*. The experience itself would bring a definite content. A believer could be so possessed by the idea of Christ that an image of him would appear visibly present, an experience utterly different from feeling a presence and then needing to interpret it.

(When I was growing up as an impressionable Roman Catholic, one of the nuns told us a story about Thomas á Kempis, the author of *The Imitation of Christ*. She said he had been considered for sainthood but, when

---

101. Ibid., 61.

his grave was opened, there was some evidence that he was trying to claw his way out after being buried alive. Thus, he was denied sainthood, either because a true saint wouldn't have tried to escape or because he had perhaps—with good reason, in my view—cursed the heavens for his hellish death. I was extremely upset by this: not only did the story tap into one of my primal terrors but it also seemed spectacularly unfair, like being denied a perfect test score because the teacher lost your last page of answers. That night, drowsing over my homework in a darkening room, I thought I saw the forlorn Thomas, taking shape in a corner, denying the suspicions and pleading with me to help him be canonized. I didn't see something weird and interpret it by what was upsetting me—like seeing a dark stain and thinking I was getting a sign. Thomas "took life" before me. The image and what it was about were part of the experience itself.)

Here's a passage from James that mentions both sorts of experiences. Notice that, for James, not the "semi-hallucinatory" images but the cases entirely without imagery are "the very highest raptures," beyond all words:

> Such manuals as Saint Ignatius's Spiritual Exercises recommend the disciple to expel sensation by a graduated series of efforts to imagine holy scenes. The acme of this kind of discipline would be a semi-hallucinatory mono-ideism—an imaginary figure of Christ, for example, coming fully to occupy the mind. Sensorial images of this sort, whether literal or symbolic, play an enormous part in mysticism. But in certain cases imagery may fall away entirely, and in the very highest raptures it tends to do so. The state of consciousness becomes then insusceptible of any verbal description. Mystical teachers are unanimous as to this.[102]

(Notice, as well, the claim of unanimity. By now, it's not surprising that on the next page he remarks: "So many men, so many minds: I imagine that these experiences can be as infinitely varied as are the idiosyncrasies of individuals."[103])

If we consider James's view of the subconscious, I think we find the same characteristics present. James seems usually to see the subconscious as the source of new forces which can enter a person's life or a region of the mind where emotional tensions can find some sort of resolution or unity. That is, he again favors experiences with as little explicit theological content as possible. However, if we take a case of conversion as James understands

---

102. Ibid., 367.
103. Ibid., 368.

it, where something comes from the periphery of consciousness to the center, it's clear that here too an idea or image could be, not an addition, but part of the experience. The most obvious example would be of someone, once religious, now an atheist, being haunted by vivid ideas which were in fact acquired in childhood and shoved to the periphery of consciousness, only to return with more power. The ideas here would be part of the experience; their entry into full consciousness is what the experience would be of. (It seems to me that this would be the case with whatever concept of the subconscious one might use.)

To qualify things even further, some of the cases James deals with as crucial examples—for example, the later experiences of Stephen Bradley[104]—occur *within* theological contexts: i.e., the people involved were already believers; yet their experience consists primarily of a resolution of an uneasiness or a sense of a comforting presence. James would like to extract the emotional turn of the experience and see the interpretation as coming in after the fact; but, for those like Bradley, belief in the Holy Spirit, visions from the Bible, and the ordinary life of a religious community—e.g., listening to sermons, prayer—were present well before the fact and could be understood as guiding the experience.

It thus seems impossible to claim religious images and theological ideas are only added to experiences, never part of them. It would seem equally impossible to claim that experiences that do contain such images and ideas are necessarily weaker or less significant. In fact, the opposite could well be argued, since the ideas and images would bring with them avenues into highly developed traditions.

What this means is that a person's religious tradition is potentially much more important than James seems willing to admit. In some cases, that tradition may not only provide a means of interpreting experience but also provide the occasion and the material of the experience itself.

James would argue, as his own use of Stephen Bradley's experiences cited above illustrates, that even when someone has definite theological beliefs, the experience of a comforting presence may not *wholly* gain its significance from the categories of a creed. Bradley calls the presence which descends on him the "Holy Spirit"—a happy choice, since it's a much less loaded name than "Christ" or "Thomas à Kempis." He says things like the following about his experience:

---

104. Ibid., 178–81.

> At first, I began to feel my heart beat very quickly all on a sudden, which made me at first think that perhaps something is going to ail me, though I was not alarmed, for I felt no pain. My heart increased in its beating, which soon convinced me that it was the Holy Spirit from the effect it had on me. I began to feel exceedingly happy and humble, and such a sense of unworthiness as I never felt before.[105]

Unlike the cases of vividly perceived ideas, this seems to be a real meeting of experience and concept. For James, this extract would be the very heart of the experience. When I first wrote on James, I thought it just possible to grant him that much. Now, for me, as I argued above, this extract would only be part of the experience and I would hesitate to call it the most, or the only, important part. But an account like Bradley's could absorb different judgments, and mark just the place independent seekers and lovers of tradition would part company.

Certainly, the quote above well represents the primary model floating through James's investigations: an experience that was vague (and perhaps kept vague by selective trimming of the account) yet still profoundly important somehow to the believer and that could be characterized by various theological descriptions. The descriptions, for James, characterize but do not create or guide or inform the experience as it happens. Here's a nice summary of his position (and note, again, the strong claim of independence, as well as the concluding claim of almost infinite flexibility):

> The transition from tenseness, self-responsibility, and worry, to equanimity, receptivity, and peace, is the most wonderful of all those shiftings of inner equilibrium, those changes of the personal centre of energy, which I have analyzed so often; and the chief wonder of it is that it so often comes about, not by doing, but by simply relaxing and throwing the burden down. This abandonment of self-responsibility seems to me the fundamental act in specifically religious, as distinguished from moral practice. It antedates theologies and is independent of philosophies. Mind-cure, theosophy, stoicism, ordinary neurological hygiene, insist on it as emphatically as Christianity does, and it is capable of entering into closest marriage with every speculative creed.[106]

---

105. Ibid., 179.
106. Ibid., 265.

In his conclusions, James makes an intriguing qualification of this point about an experience in some way bearing its own significance:

> Although the religious question is primarily a question of life, of living or not living in the higher union which opens itself to us as a gift, yet the spiritual excitement in which the gift appears a real one will often fail to be aroused in an individual until certain particular beliefs or ideas which, as we say, come home to him, are touched.[107]

In other words, without some sort of expression beyond the experience, without some beliefs or ideas active in the person, the gift may never appear a real one:

> These ideas will thus be essential to that individual's religion;—which is as much to say that over-beliefs in various directions are absolutely indispensable, and that we should treat them with tenderness and tolerance so long as they are not intolerant themselves.[108]

But, and here is the point that goes along with James's idea of a vague but significant experience, there is *no particular creed* which can be said to provide a basic description of this sort of experience: in the immediate encounter, most any creed will suffice if only it does preserve the importance of the experience and does allow the individual to be touched.

This passage highlights as well one of James's primary concerns and one of the things that drew me most to *The Varieties*: James's tolerance, sustained by the denial that any particular tradition has an exclusive right to speak for religion. It remains one of the most attractive parts of *The Varieties*, and it's worth stressing that James understands himself as defending not the diversity of creeds but the diversity of human lives that need them:

> If an Emerson were forced to be a Wesley, or a Moody forced to be a Whitman, the total human consciousness of the divine would suffer. The divine can mean no single quality, it must mean a group of qualities, by being champions of which in alternation, different men may all find worthy missions. Each attitude being a syllable in human nature's total message, it takes the whole of us to spell the meaning out completely. . . . We must frankly recognize the fact

---

107. Ibid., 459.
108. Ibid., 459–60.

that we live in partial systems and that parts are not interchangeable in the spiritual life.[109]

William James, as this clearly shows, is the prophet not of religious life but of all human life.

As I said above, my younger self wanted to grant James more than I would now. The idea of an experience that in itself was of religious significance seems much less plausible to me and much more in need of qualification to be salvaged at all. Even accepting a set of such experiences and granting their vitality, one would end up excluding a large number of experiences that most people would call religious, experiences that would seem just as vital. One would also be ignoring other elements in the religious life that are powerful sources of vision and strength. This will become clear when we turn to the third assumption and ask in what sense the kind of experience James values can be the foundation of all religious life.

3/ Foundation

I've come to think this issue loomed much larger for me than it ever did for James. For him, it was such a deep assumption that the powerful experiences of individuals were the creative source of religion that he never seriously felt the need to argue for it. Moreover, he could see no serious alternative. For me, it was something I hoped could be argued for and established. I had lived in the alternative my entire life: a world-wide, tradition-heavy, dictatorial community I was hoping to escape. James was happy to assume the independence and the primacy of individuals. I wanted to prove James right; yet this became the point at which I concluded he was most crucially wrong.

So: In what sense does James claim that individual religious experience is the foundation of the religious life?

Just as God could be said both to bring creation into existence and to sustain creation in existence continually, the experience of a saint, a mystic, or a redeemed sinner might either begin a tradition or keep a tradition vibrant through constant renewal. How does James see it working?

In his first lecture, as we saw, James first claims his psychological standpoint dictates he concern himself with the religious individual. Yet, as he defends his concentration on troubled, violent, and haunted people, he

---

109. Ibid., 437.

appeals not to his methodology but to what he considers to be the nature of true religion:

> There can be no doubt that as a matter of fact a religious life, exclusively pursued, does tend to make the person exceptional and eccentric. I speak now not of your ordinary religious believer, who follows the conventional observances of his country, whether it be Buddhist, Christian, or Mohammedan. His religion has been made for him by others, communicated to him by tradition, determined to fixed forms by imitation, and retained by habit. It would profit us little to study this secondhand life. We must make search rather for the original experiences which were the pattern-setters to all this mass of suggested feeling and imitated conduct. These experiences we can only find in individuals for whom religion exists not as a dull habit, but as an acute fever rather.[110]

Look at the contrast James has drawn. The "original experiences" of individuals for whom religion exists "as an acute fever" are "the pattern-setters" for the ordinary believer, whose religion "has been made for him" by those individuals. The religious life of the ordinary believer is a "dull habit," a "secondhand life" of "suggested feeling and imitated conduct." Taken at its strongest, this passage would imply that no one who followed a religious tradition could possibly lead an authentic religious life; anyone who did would originate a new pattern, create a new tradition—as Jesus, Luther, or Wesley did.

This line of argument is primarily a claim about the literal beginning of the religious life: a chronological claim about the primacy of individual experience, together with a dismissal of those who come after the founder.

But *did* Jesus, Luther, Wesley and all the other great religious figures originate new patterns or create new traditions? In the strong sense James describes, surely not. All these "founders" inherited a great part of the faith they lived. Luther and Wesley obviously rose up within highly developed traditional communities based on the way of Christ, which they explicitly wanted to follow. They studied and sought to imitate other figures of that tradition, notably Augustine and Paul. Even Jesus inherited the faith of Israel, including the role of prophet and teacher, worshiped in the synagogue, revered the temple. They all drew heavily on their traditions.

More strongly still, there are clear cases of powerful figures, as much filled with faith as Luther and Wesley, who yet did not "found" other sects:

110. Ibid., 15.

St. Francis of Assisi and St. Teresa would be obvious examples. If one objects that St. Francis, say, did form a new order of monks, then take three of the strongest religious figures of my youth: Daniel Berrigan, a Jesuit priest; Thomas Merton, a Cistercian hermit; and Martin Luther King, Jr., a Baptist pastor. No one could claim that religion for them was anything less than an acute fever: yet they founded no new traditions, but acted faithfully within the traditions they had. (Merton, the convert, went looking for a tradition to lose himself in.)

There thus seems little defense for the kind of claim James set out. If any of his position can be salvaged, it would be by understanding the primacy of such figures as a sustaining, rather than creating or originating, power. Recall James's statement of what he calls the religious problem:

> Here is the real core of the religious problem: Help! help! No prophet can claim to bring a final message unless he says things that will have a sound of reality in the ears of victims such as these. But the deliverance must come in as strong a form as the complaint, if it is to take effect; and that seems a reason why the coarser religions, revivalistic, orgiastic, with blood and miracles and supernatural operations, may possibly never be displaced.[111]

That is, we might grant that the concepts and practices which make sense of religious experience are handed down by tradition independently of these experiences and still claim that what keeps the tradition going is the constant return to experience by the individuals of that tradition, the ability of a Luther, a Wesley, and a Fox to be *possessed* by the ideas of their tradition. The religious life would thus be continually renewed and sustained by believers who filled the propositions of faith with the passions of faith.

Certainly, all serious believers can name people from their lives who inspired them and helped form the faith they have, who gave them what James would call the particular "go" of their religion. I doubt if I would have even considered a life of church service if Berrigan, Merton, and King had not made such an impact on me.

Yet, here again, that impact itself no doubt gained its strength from my having grown up within a Christian community. I had been given by others the ears to hear these messages. Still, if any case can be made for individual experience to be the foundation of religious life, it would seem to be along these lines.

111. Ibid., 151.

But, once we have placed James's claim on this ground, it's open to another attack, one that is also based on experience: experience not individual and solitary but communal, the experience of being part of a community in its worship and work together.

When I was a very young Roman Catholic, before the days of Vatican II, a typical church service went something like this: the priest and the acolytes were the official congregation, conducting the entire service in Latin (spoken so low as to be inaudible past the communion rail), while members of the congregation a/ said the rosary, b/ recited litanies to special saints for special favors, c/ prayed free-style, or d/ went round the church following the stations of the cross. Thus, whatever approach to God took place in such a setting was conceived on a wholly individual basis—the Mass, the Latin chants, the incense, provided a background, a *basso continuo*, for one's own personal devotion, carried on in isolation from the other believers. In the eyes of the Second Vatican Council, this was not only a mess from the aesthetic point of view, it was a perversion of the *kind* of religious experience the Mass was designed to be; communal worship and ritual were meant to provide experiences at least as important in the total fabric of the religious life as what goes on between an individual and God. James admits the *aesthetic* value of ritual to some temperaments and acknowledges that it might form an important part of someone's religion.[112] But this is too weak an admission. The point is not that a communal ritual is an individual experience of an aesthetically different sort; it's that, unless we stretch the word "individual" beyond all useful bounds, such a ritual is not an individual experience at all. It can be used as such, and has been, but at its heart is something else.

Religious communities don't lack those who would insist communal experience *alone* forms, and ought to form, the foundation of the religious life. During the years of my service, I probably heard Christmas Eve candlelight services, Easter sunrise services, revival meetings, and church camp experiences cited most often as experiences both valuable in themselves and foundational for faith. (To be honest, I still find some of this massed-togetherness a little oppressive. I've wondered if this were only a difference in eras, of different needs and expectations. I find it intriguing that the communal experiences I listed are more typically of joy than of desperation.) But my point isn't to decide for one over the other: what is of importance is that we are faced with the well-taken claim that worship

---

112. Ibid., 411–14.

rituals, carried on in a nonindividualistic manner, as well as communal experiences of other sorts, are at least as important to the religious life as individual religious experiences, the *"experiences of individual men in their solitude."*[113] Even limiting the sense of "foundation," religious experience as James understands it has a serious rival.

All three assumptions I thought *The Varieties* rested on thus turned out to be defensible only in an extremely limited sense. It seemed impossible to me to dismiss as "secondhand" living as much of the religious life as James wanted to. Deciding he was wrong changed the way I thought about religion.

I'm not sure, however, that criticizing James's assumptions as I've done would have bothered him that much. I can almost hear him making one of his blithe reversals, agreeing that of course he'd overstated the case and of course there was much more to be said about . . . well, about everything. (I fear I must admit that this happy style of extravagant advance and generous retreat may be one of the ways James has affected my thinking most.)

But, as I said, this was an issue that loomed large for me. I had taken up *The Varieties* to study religion, and I had wanted James to be right. But James himself didn't set out to say something about religion; he set out to say something about life. I've sometimes thought the title and subtitle of the lectures could be reversed: *A Study of Human Nature: Illustrated by a Variety of Religious Experiences.*

It's the particular people James selects from religious history that seem to him important witnesses to human life and possibility. From this point of view, James can be seen as stretching the boundaries of religion, pushing it beyond its own understandings, reminding it of larger horizons, reminding it of its part in the human story.

This is something most religious communities usually need reminding of. James and the rough community he gathered remained with me over the years as ever present warnings against narrow demands, absolute divisions, inflexible boundaries. They helped me see the messy breadth of human feeling and acting. I could almost hear the whisper in my ear: "Well, yes, of course, you have a point, but don't forget . . ."

I think this was his intent, an intent deeper than his assumptions, something that transforms his study into a disguised sermon: to present a spiritual vanguard that would call us beyond ourselves. It's what he saw

113. Ibid., 36.

in the saints, who turned out to be just the sort of people James hoped his philosophy might produce.

5. Saints in the Hands of an Empirical Philosopher

I have come to think of James's lectures on "The Value of Saintliness" as the climax and the true conclusion of *The Varieties*. Here the story James has been telling (or searching for) clarifies itself and we see the lives he admires and the lives he scorns. We see how we might live and bear the fruits of goodness. He says, when he begins these lectures, that he is turning from description to appreciation.[114] But no one can read the preceding lectures on "Saintliness" as anything close to neutral description: he's gathering up his heroic exemplars, the pioneers of our salvation. James claims to be offering an evaluation of the saints, but it strikes me as more a proclamation. Here is what we're really meant to contemplate in *The Varieties*.

When I reread these sections for this project, I thought they might rank as the finest things James ever wrote. They're crucial for understanding his approach to moral and religious issues. They contain a powerful defense of empiricism as a way of sorting out human values. The lectures are written with an easy union of nimble wit and vivid examples. They show, better than some of the more famous essays, the fascination with particular lives and characters that lay behind all of his ethical writings. They show his heart and the human qualities that called to him most deeply.

At the very beginning of the ostensibly descriptive lectures on "Saintliness," James puts the final judgment of his entire investigation in one concentrated statement: "the best fruits of religious experience are the best things that history has to show."[115] It's worth underlining that he presents these fruits not as *religion's* best, but *history's* best, the peak of human life as such. And he follows this judgment immediately with a revealing characterization that shows more precisely what it is he admires: "here if anywhere is the genuinely strenuous life."[116] It's the ascetic character, with its warrior-like self-sacrifice, that appeals to him most. He ends both the "Saintliness" and "The Value of Saintliness" lectures with a denunciation of modern materialism and an encomium to the strenuous life and the virtue of poverty. It's more than fitting that, when James is illustrating the virtue

---

114. Ibid., 299.
115. Ibid., 239.
116. Ibid.

of charity, he chooses one of the most violent and pugnacious characters in his gallery, Richard Weaver, a miner and semi-pro boxer, who broke the jaw of a man who called him a coward for refusing, as a Christian, to fight him. James quotes a long passage from his biography, where Weaver, having overcome his demons, shames a bully by literally turning the other cheek and allowing the man to pummel his face. The next day, weeping, the bully asks his forgiveness.[117]

It's more than a strong example of forgiveness and non-resistance: the physical violence and the surging passions show clearly what ignites James's interest and admiration. He closes the passage by crying out, "Love your enemies!" But Weaver's nonresistance does more than this, and it's something that will also enter James's judgment of the saint's value: more than simply returning his enemy good for evil, Weaver's turning the cheek *transforms* his enemy through a moral force.

It's no surprise that what James finds most infuriating in religious life is its decline into trivial concerns and polite routines. After noting that athletics, militarism(!), enterprise, and adventure, unlike contemporary religion, are "remarkable for the energy with which they make for heroic standards of life,"[118] he adds this footnote:

> "When a church has to be run by oysters, ice-cream, and fun," I read in an American religious paper, "you may be sure that it is running away from Christ." Such, if one may judge by appearances, is the present plight of many of our churches.[119]

Like Weaver's pugilism, the phrase "oysters, ice-cream, and fun" carries an edge of scorn for polite society that James finds irresistible. He happily quotes Emerson ridiculing Unitarianism with a violent image I'm sure he also found irresistible:

> Luther, says Emerson, would have cut off his right hand rather than nail his theses to the door at Wittenberg, if he had supposed that they were destined to lead to the pale negations of Boston Unitarianism.[120]

When I was young, I laughed along with James and delighted in the same ridicule. At the time, I thought the real passions of faith could only

---

117. Ibid., 258–59.
118. Ibid., 331.
119. Ibid.
120. Ibid., 302.

lead to Martin Luther King's prophetic calls for justice or Daniel Berrigan's denunciations of war. When I gave the lecture at my Lutheran seminary, reprinted here as Part Two, and used the above quote, I got the biggest laugh of the morning.

Today, with religious mutilations and twisted minds too vivid a presence in the world around me, I pull out this quote to illustrate the different world James wrote in. I imagine most of the world's people, if asked today, what religious passion was most likely to lead to, would answer: bigotry and brutality; violence against women and gays; the careless, random killings of terrorism. I imagine, familiar with this horrific alternative, they would see the decline of religion into ice-cream and fun as a matter for delirious celebration.

Since William James hated both cruelty and the deadly certainties of dogmatism, it isn't hard to guess what he would think about our poisonous climate. And he was certainly aware of and sensitive to the reality of religious fanaticism and the distortions of devotion. But there's a sense in *The Varieties* that we might be past all this primitive barbarism, perhaps because of the waning power of religious institutions. In fact, James is quite willing to lay all the horrors of religious behavior at the feet of those institutions. Here's a powerful statement of this judgment, and note his characteristic outrage at "human neophobia," the fear of the new and different:

> The basenesses so commonly charged to religion's account are thus, almost all of them, not chargeable at all to religion proper, but rather to religion's wicked practical partner, the spirit of corporate dominion. And the bigotries are most of them in their turn chargeable to religion's wicked intellectual partner, the spirit of dogmatic dominion, the passion for laying down the law in the form of an absolutely closed-in theoretic system. . . . The baiting of Jews, the hunting of Albigenses and Waldenses, the stoning of Quakers and ducking of Methodists, the murdering of Mormons and the massacring of Armenians, express much rather that aboriginal human neophobia, that pugnacity of which we all share the vestiges, and that inborn hatred of the alien and of eccentric and non-conforming men as aliens, than they express the positive piety of the various perpetrators. Piety is the mask, the inner force is tribal instinct.[121]

James will himself qualify this one-sided judgment when he discusses the extremes of devotion, admitting that the saintly temper in itself is vulnerable

---

121. Ibid., 308.

to fanaticism.¹²² Yet we see throughout the discussion of saintliness and its value one particular grouping of experience and action that James is defining and defending, as though he were separating the promising students, his favorites, from a mostly indifferent, or even dangerous, class. It's the fruit of that deepest of his assumptions I analyzed in the preceding section, the "originally innocent thing" which is corrupted by "the spirit of politics and the lust of dogmatic rule," the experience "which lives itself out within the private breast."¹²³ It is not simply the independence and the individualism that appeal to James, but the sense of new adventure in this experience:

> Naked comes it into the world, and lonely; and it has always, for a time at least, driven him who had it into the wilderness, often into the literal wilderness out of doors, where the Buddha, Jesus, Mohammed, St. Francis, George Fox, and so many others had to go.¹²⁴

James follows this declaration with a long passage from George Fox's journal, describing his passage through a wilderness both literal and spiritual. Despite Fox's torment, this passage is for James, not simply the illustration of a point, but the description of a life worth living.

I quoted in the last section James's "composite photograph of universal saintliness" when I was discussing his efforts to find one core experience, common to all faiths. It's worth quoting this passage again as a defining of the object of his judgment of value. And notice, this time, the expansive, benevolent atmosphere James sees in the experience of the saints, as well as the strong impetus toward self-denial and self-sacrifice:

1. A feeling of being in a wider life than that of this world's selfish little interests; and a conviction, not merely intellectual, but as it were sensible, of the existence of an Ideal Power . . .
2. A sense of the friendly continuity of the ideal power with our own life, and a willing self-surrender to its control.
3. An immense elation and freedom, as the outlines of the confining selfhood melt down.
4. A shifting of the emotional centre towards loving and harmonious affections, toward "yes, yes," and away from "no," where the claims of the non-ego are concerned.¹²⁵

---

122. Ibid., 312.
123. Ibid., 306.
124. Ibid.
125. Ibid., 249–50.

It's clear from this list that some of what James valued in the saints and mystics was the richness and breadth they revealed in human experience: the petty self joining an Ideal Power, melting into a wider, friendly life, filled with elation and freedom, turning outward in love. This might seem an almost too happy picture of a universe James usually depicts more harshly. But that's the point: the saint's experience brings a revelation of light into the world's usual darkness. Also, James immediately sharpens and toughens his picture by adding four "characteristic practical consequences": asceticism, strength of soul, purity, and charity.[126] I would guess that most people, merely reading that list, would be struck less by inviting warmth than by challenging demands. Here's how James fleshes out that list: "self-surrender may become so passionate as to turn into self-immolation"; "personal motives . . . become too insignificant for notice"; "weaknesses of the flesh are treated with relentless severity"; "The saint . . . treats loathsome beggars as his brothers."[127]

This expansive, demanding life that James sketches is, for him, the very distillation of the religious life, and it's this that James will pronounce to be of great value, both to individuals and to all humanity. Furthermore, it's this life that will advance the cause of any gods in the universe worth serving.

Before we look at James's judgment on the saints in detail, it's important to note the serious limitations on the scope of this judgment.

As I argued in the last section, no simple claims about either the autonomy or the originality of religious experience can be sustained. More pointedly, religious traditions and communal experiences play a far greater and far more positive role in the lives of believers, even James's heroes, like Francis and Luther, than James is willing to admit. He sees the oppression of institutions, not their powers of renewal and inspiration. (In the same way, he sees the expansive possibilities of individuals and is reluctant to admit their oppressive impulses.) When James pronounces on the fruits of religion, he's hardly judging the worth of religion itself but the worth of a certain sort of experience which is neither the only nor the only important sort of religious experience. Moreover, as he sifts through the saints and their qualities, even some of those who seem to exemplify his ideal type of religious experience turn out to be much less fruitful than others.

126. Ibid., 251.
127. Ibid.

I don't mean to trivialize what James has done, only to get a clearer sense of it. I've come to think of *The Varieties* as less a study of religion than James's major, and spectacularly vivid, work on ethics.

Now let's look at how James comes to his evaluation.

I discussed earlier James's distinction between an existential and a spiritual judgment, and explored some of the problems with the former. I noted also that, although he gave three criteria for the spiritual judgment, he would never systematically use them. In fact, when he does come to discuss the value of saintliness, he refers only to the rough standard of "common sense," not to the criteria he originally set out.[128] Still, let's examine those criteria. If they're not systematically used, they still lay behind most of what he says, and calling them "common sense" is fair enough:

> When we think certain states of mind superior to others, is it ever because of what we know concerning their organic antecedents? No! It is always for two entirely different reasons. It is either because we take an immediate delight in them; or else it is because we believe them to bring us good consequential fruits for life.[129]

The latter criterion turns out to have two sides to it, however, and we are left finally with the following:

> ... spiritual judgments [are] judgments based on our own immediate feeling primarily; and secondarily on what we can ascertain of their experiential relations to our moral needs and to the rest of what we hold as true.
> *Immediate luminousness*, in short, *philosophical reasonableness*, and *moral helpfulness* are the only available criteria.[130]

Let's try to separate what James usually mixes together and see what each implies.

1/ Immediate Luminousness

It's very tempting to see these three criteria as a reformulation of the three parts of the pragmatic theory of truth: a/ accounting for the facts; b/ harmonizing with other truths; c/ leading investigation in fruitful directions. Certainly, the criteria for evaluating saintliness show the same feeling for

---

128. Ibid., 300.
129. Ibid., 22.
130. Ibid., 24-25.

the complexity of human investigation and judgment, but seeing why they're different will give us a clearer view of them, especially of the first. James is primarily concerned here not with how and why we judge statements to be true but with how and why we find experiences valuable. The issue of truth is an important part of this, as we'll see in discussing the second criterion, but evaluating the truth of knowledge claims is not the same as evaluating the worth or importance of an experience. And it's the first criterion, immediate luminousness, that's definitive here: a religious experience may or may not be used as evidence for some fact but finding or declaring an experience immediately luminous does not constitute such a use. We don't immediately feel that "such and such is the case" but that the experience we're undergoing is "good" or "important" or "overwhelming" or "uplifting." (Again, the question of truth will come up but not under the first criterion.) Most importantly, we're not judging a proposition but evaluating an experience (or, as James says, a state of mind).

Drunkenness is a good example of what James has in mind here. Judged immediately, the experience of being drunk seems much more pleasant than an ordinary state of mind. Thus, it is "immediately luminous," not in the sense that we immediately perceive some fact but in the sense that we spontaneously place a (perhaps extreme, perhaps illusory) value on it, either by simply delighting in it or by feeling it to be an important, vital experience. Such a state of mind could be said to contain or lead to a judgment, even a very simple one like "this is good"; but it's not necessary that this judgment be consciously articulated for the state of mind to be immediately luminous: it's only necessary that the subject be consciously enjoying it or feeling its value. So: religious experiences are immediately luminous because those who have them feel they are somehow tremendously important, perhaps the most important experiences they've ever had.

But an interesting issue arises here connected to whom the judgment is being made by. For a mystic, the judgment thus far is an experience; for anyone else, James or me, say, it's a *report*. Again, there's a crucial and revealing difference with the pragmatic theory of truth: there, the first step, accounting for the facts, must be publicly available, even allowing for debate about what constitutes a fact, in a way a powerful experience is not. There could obviously be different judgments made by insider and outsider. Also, just how the judgment is articulated will matter greatly when we turn to the criterion of philosophical reasonableness.

Here's where things get interesting. James was comfortable seeing the immediate use, or presence, of concepts in the religious experience as a kind of poetic act; there really was no one set of concepts which were more adequate than another for the type of experience that interested him, so long as whatever concepts were used preserved the sacred dimensions of the experience. Taken this way, the immediate judgment is not a judgment in a rigorous sense, but an expression of the importance of the experience to the individual. But the later stages of the spiritual judgment, which James calls the "more remote" criteria,[131] are both more rigorous and more enmeshed in our common life and thought; thus, they necessitate the articulation of that immediate judgment in a way the first stage does not: we move from evaluating an experience to testing statements about that experience. Thus, any differences in expressing or describing that immediate experience will take on more importance as we proceed. With his commitment to a certain kind of experience he considers primary, James has to take some care in choosing which propositions are to be judged against the second criterion. We'll see what he comes up with in section six. Right now, let's see what the next criterion involves.

2/ Philosophical Reasonableness

Less immediate, less intimately bound to moment and feeling, the criterion of philosophical reasonableness should place insider and outsider on the same ground, testing whether or not the immediate judgment evoked by the experience accords with our other beliefs about the world. Drunkenness, again, is a simple example of the tension. Suppose one night while intoxicated someone declares "Being drunk all day is the best thing that could happen to a person!" If we take that as a claim about the supreme goodness of that immediate experience, we see how poorly it harmonizes with other things we know about alcohol and health, and thus how philosophically unreasonable it is.

Religious experience, of course, is more complex and presents the two serious difficulties I noted above. First, if the spiritual judgment is being made by someone who has not had what could strictly speaking be called a religious experience, the original experience seems so remote from our ordinary experience that the primary judgments of those who have had such experiences might seem suspect. Second, the primary judgments, even at

---

131. Ibid., 23.

their simplest, usually imply claims about the larger nature of life and the universe, which are much more difficult to evaluate than claims about alcohol. If the notion of religious experience is as varied and complex as we have found it, which claims are we to choose if we are judging religious experience as a whole? James, as we've seen, wants to keep these immediate claims as theologically vague as possible; others would insist they must be richer. Obviously, the more specific and detailed the claim, the more challenging the test.

But let's ask how we'd go about doing this at all: What sorts of considerations are relevant to determining the philosophical reasonableness of the immediate judgment?

To meet the first difficulty, the remoteness of religious experience from ordinary experience, is something James tries to overcome with the "nonreligious" examples he scatters through the book. As I argued when discussing his psychological standpoint, things like drunkenness and drug-induced trances are meant to throw light on certain formal aspects of religious experience, e.g., the way a mystic's self seems to open up and enter a deeper realm. But these examples also serve to open the mind of James's audience. To call up extreme, expansive experiences, which are yet familiar to most of us, makes religious experiences, though strange, more reasonable:

> Most of us can remember the strangely moving power of passages in certain poems read when we were young, irrational doorways as they were through which the mystery of fact, the wildness and the pang of life, stole into our hearts and thrilled them.[132]

Without claiming that all the things he brings up are of a specifically religious nature (and they may be more effective if they are not), he is trying to loosen our notions of what is possible, to create some sympathy for the sincere reporting of so odd an occurrence as a religious experience. This, it seems to me, is part of the general impact of the work as a whole, and I think James is largely successful in this particular attempt.

However, the most important task connected to this criterion is ascertaining if the immediate judgment harmonizes with what we know of the rest of the world. James takes this wider horizon very broadly, including not only our current understanding of how the world works, but the values and ideals we currently treasure, and his heart is very much with the second.

---

132. Ibid., 345.

Nevertheless, he can hardly avoid the narrower consideration of how religious claims are related to scientific investigations, and an issue James worked very hard to exclude from the spiritual judgment inevitably returns: the *origin* of those religious states of mind he's been describing.

The optimum case would be if we could verify that the judgment based on immediate luminousness was correct, e.g., if we could establish that you did encounter something that was first in being and power. But there must be at least a possibility of truth; the judgment must not contradict any of our other beliefs or, if it does contradict one or several of them, those beliefs must not be strongly verified. And, in the case of religious experience, one of the crucial questions involved would have to be: is there at least a possibility that the experience was a real connection with a power greater than ourselves, something at least god-*like* but something definitely other and greater than us? So, even for the spiritual judgment, we can't simply dismiss the medical materialists as irrelevant. We can't say it makes *no* difference whether what they claim is true or not. James clearly had doubts about the truth of the medical materialist position; but it's important to see that the question can't be avoided.

Still, it's the larger dimension of philosophical reasonableness, how religious claims relate to our deepest needs, our moral yearnings, our passionate aspirations, and our desperate battles, that grips James most strongly. It's this that James uses to sort out both the human qualities he admires and the divinities he respects. Very early on in the lectures, James began comparing religious points of view by asking if they left any essential human needs unsatisfied: the reason morbid-mindedness was superior to healthy-mindedness was that it gave full recognition to human pain and suffering.

All through the lectures on saintliness and those on its value, we see James doing this to the saints and their gods, measuring them by the breadth or narrowness of their characters, the good they do or fail to do for those around them, how cruel or how loving they are. It seems to me he puts much more energy and passion into these discussions than he can summon up for the abstract discussions of truth that conclude *The Varieties*.

In fact, at the conclusion of "The Value of Saintliness" lectures, when he finally prepares to turn to the narrower question of truth, he can't help sounding dismissive, seeming to imply that such an issue would only be raised by the rather pedantic defenders of religion and is not, strictly speaking, part of his inquiry:

> How, you say, can religion, which believes in two worlds and an invisible order, be estimated by the adaptation of its fruits to this world's order alone? It is its *truth*, not its utility, you insist, upon which our verdict ought to depend.[133]

Notice: it's "you," not James, who is saying and insisting this.

Finally, though, after considering mysticism and philosophy as means of certifying the truth of religion, he concludes:

> We have wound our way back, after our excursion through mysticism and philosophy, to where we were before: the uses of religion, its uses to the individual who has it, and the uses of the individual himself to the world, are the best arguments that truth is in it. We return to the empirical philosophy: the true is what works well.[134]

I almost laughed out loud when I re-read that last sentence, remembering the gory history of the pragmatic theory of truth and impressed again by James's unrepentant bluntness.

Writing as a serious young philosophy grad student, I saw *The Varieties* as driving toward the issue of truth, and I took at face value James's claims that he was doing just that. I suspect now that what he was doing could be better described as putting off an issue he'd rather not deal with and occupying himself with things he found much more interesting.

I rushed, in the earlier version of this writing, to insist that James himself, whenever forced to defend his writings on truth, always included less exotic notions of that concept within his notion of "working well." I pointed out that James's apparent disclaimers stemmed from the failure to apply his own standards systematically. More to the point, I noted that all the second criterion required on this score was the *possibility* of truth and that James would do his best to provide that in his final lecture (which, again, seeing this myself as the most important issue, I saved for my final section). All this was correct, as far as it went.

But now I think I was seriously missing the point of what was going on. Certainly I missed the force of the above statement and its focus on what happens in a person's life and world. I'm afraid I had a hard time thinking "philosophical reasonableness" could legitimately mean anything but "consistent with the current stage of scientific thought." I knew, and yet failed to grasp sufficiently, that James didn't simply slip into a discussion of

---

133. Ibid., 341.
134. Ibid., 411.

moral vision while he should have been discussing truth; he was thinking along those lines from the beginning. I misjudged the weight he instinctively gave his criteria.

It would be absurd to say that James was uninterested in what religion might have to tell about the universe; but he was most interested in, and primarily searched through, all those testimonies of believers for what they might say about human life, that most interesting part of the universe.

3/ Moral Helpfulness

This criterion is strongly bound to the wider aspect of philosophical reasonableness. And, like the first criterion, this shows clearly he's not formulating a reasonably defensible theory about religion, but evaluating lives and the world shaped by those lives. However, unlike immediate luminousness, the judgment of moral helpfulness is more remote than immediate, not made during or within the experience; it's an attempt to weigh the experience in a broader context, to ascertain how far the experience might move saint, community, and world toward the ideals that in part constitute what is philosophically reasonable at any given time. It's a judgment of the force and the power of the experience in the life itself, and the power of the life in both act and example.

It's easy to see how there might be tensions between the first two criteria, the tension, put crudely, between feeling and fact. In James's own words:

> What immediately feels most "good" is not always most "true," when measured by the verdict of the rest of experience. The difference between Philip drunk and Philip sober is the classic instance in corroboration. If merely "feeling good" could decide, drunkenness would be the supremely valid human experience.[135]

(This was the prime tension I envisioned when I first wrote on James. I thought most thinkers would grant that religious experience might be tremendously powerful and productive of fine human beings and yet deny it had any divine or supernatural source.)

It might seem, at first, that there might potentially be less discordance between the first and third criteria. An expansive experience might shape an expansive personality, though nothing supernatural was involved. But

---

135. Ibid., 23.

the moral effects of experience need not harmonize at all. Here is James again, continuing with drunkenness:

> The sway of alcohol over mankind is unquestionably due to its power to stimulate the mystical faculties of human nature, usually crushed to earth by the cold facts and dry criticisms of the sober hour. . . . To the poor and unlettered it stands in the place of symphony concerts and of literature; and it is part of the deeper mystery and tragedy of life that whiffs and gleams of something that we immediately recognized as excellent should be vouchsafed to so many of us only in the fleeting earlier phases of what in its totality is so degrading a poisoning.[136]

It's more than "cold fact" that brings the tension here: degradation is a moral effect, the destruction of character and, beyond that, the whole fabric of a life and its relationships.

Thus, the same violent tension could exist between the immediate and remote effects of religious experience, beyond the issue of factual truth; intoxication *with God* might lead in a multitude of directions: from breathtaking personal sacrifice to peaceful bliss to mass murder. Where suicide bombers are celebrated, all might be claimed at once. Where suicide bombers are condemned, the deadly fruits alone are a damning judgment on the faith of the bombers and, for some, on religion itself. In other words, not only might there be violent tensions within the religious judgment, there are wildly varying possibilities in its application. I concluded this section of my early version by saying: "In other words, there just may be no simple judgment possible." As I write now, I wonder if James's enterprise was more deeply embedded in the outlook of his era than I could have imagined, founded on the encyclopedic aspirations of an international community of learning. I wonder how sensible any judgment of religion as such can be.

Of course, James is as aware of varieties of judgment as he is of varieties of experience. When he begins his lectures on "The Value of Saintliness," instead of employing his explicit criteria, he says our only guides can be: "our general philosophic prejudices, our instincts, and our common sense."[137] I would take those as a fair summary of his formal criteria, and they imply both a rough weighing of disparate parts and a recognized evolution of standards. But James primarily wants us to engage our sense of what is morally and aesthetically valuable. Thus, when he wants an example

---

136. Ibid., 349.
137. Ibid., 299–300.

of a god that common sense would instinctively reject, he doesn't cite one with naively pictured spatiotemporal qualities but one with a repulsive *character*.

This is an important stance and very characteristic of James. The usual clash of religion with science and philosophy, the long modern debate over the solar system and the evolution of species, is a clash of world-views, about what's in the world and how it all works. James sees this as well as any modern thinker, but he's gripped by something else. A god sitting on a cloud hurling thunderbolts down at little creatures seems to advancing science progressively more implausible. To James, anything hurling thunderbolts and killing the helpless seems cruel and disgusting, and he would claim this perception as *moral* progress. He argues strongly that our moral values shift as surely as our cosmological pictures do, and for the same reason: our experience of the world and our evolving attempts to understand it and live in it.

Here's one of my favorite passages on this issue:

> The monarchical type of sovereignty was, for example, so ineradicably planted in the mind of our own forefathers that a dose of cruelty and arbitrariness in their deity seems positively to have been required by their imagination. They called the cruelty "retributive justice," and a God without it would certainly have struck them as not sovereign enough. But today we abhor the very notion of eternal suffering inflicted; and that arbitrary dealing out of salvation and damnation to selected individuals, of which Jonathan Edwards could persuade himself that he had not only a conviction, but a "delightful conviction," as of a doctrine "exceeding pleasant, bright and sweet," appears to us, if sovereignly anything, sovereignly irrational and mean.[138]

It seems to me that this is one of the great strengths of *The Varieties*, and of James's work as a whole: the refusal to reject human notions of value when dealing with religion, the refusal to be intimidated by absolute claims of authority. T.S. Eliot famously said that Henry James had a mind so fine no idea could violate it. The same receptivity to experience, the ability to shape thought and theory without distorting experience, made William James fairly immune to dogmatism.

James used this passage as part of his argument that theological systems themselves evolve under the pressure of experience, thus undercutting

---

138. Ibid., 301–2.

their claims of unchanging standards; it also clearly marks his judgment of where our current moral standards are. Reading it now, a half-century after I was first nodding along with it happily, I'm amazed at how distant the world James is speaking for seems. I would find it impossible now to state without qualification: "today we abhor the very notion of eternal suffering inflicted." It seems that fewer and fewer of us do. Jonathan Edwards's attitude would appear untroublingly normal in today's American Christian world: "we" hardly abhor either the delight in eternal suffering, as justified vengeance, or the willingness to inflict cruelty. I think the U.S. military wouldn't have embraced torture so easily without the impact of the punitive, self-righteous faith of the self-styled evangelical Christians. In the same year I'm writing this, a U.S. senator, in a senate discussion about the prisoners at Guantanamo, said he was opposed to their release because he thought they should rot in hell but, since they weren't there yet, he wanted them to rot in Guantanamo. I can't recall anyone saying that his statement was an expression of irrational and mean cruelty that had no place among "us." It's become too characteristic of us.

By measuring my time against James's, I'm not implying that James would have any problems deciding what he thought about our cruelty or that he would be surprised at the mere shifting of the moral sense. I do think, however, that he might be surprised by its shifting for the worse. More importantly, as *The Varieties* is a fairly positive argument for the value to the human community of a fairly passionate form of religious experience and life, I think the regaining of power by the religions of the world and the reappearance of cruelty and bigotry in their public action seriously limits the scope of his over-all judgment even further. This is what has made me see *The Varieties*, as I said above, less as a study of religion, in any plausible sense, and more as James's own call to the Good Life.

James's claim that all systems of belief, without exception, are reached from human experience is as unlikely to convince the absolutists of our day as it was the absolutists of his. But since the absolutists use the mere assertion of unchanging truth and unquestionable sacred authority when all their real arguments crumble, James's voice is, if anything, even more important to hear in our time:

> The deity to whom the prophets, seers, and devotees who founded the particular cult bore witness was worth something to them personally. They could use him. . . . In any case, they chose him for the value of the fruits he seemed to them to yield. . . . Religions have

> *approved* themselves; they have ministered to sundry vital needs which they found reigning. When they violated other needs too strongly, or when other faiths came which served the same needs better, the first religions were supplanted.[139]

In other words, the cruel gods have come among us again because cruel people needed them.

I want to focus James's position with one more point. James obviously finds the idea of eternal punishment repugnant, and one can imagine an equally obvious challenge: What difference does it make whether James likes the idea or not, if in fact such a punishment awaits him? James himself raises some hypothetical variations of this question, and he's usually tempted to answer easily along the lines I've sketched above: beliefs have always changed as we've changed. But there's a deeper answer lying behind his explicit arguments and it's bound to his moral passion: the difference James hating eternal punishment makes is that he doesn't have to worship any deity that threatened it, real or not. The vital issue is settling on which god or gods *deserve* worship. Isolated fanatics and authoritarian leaders claim to accept their harsh divinities just because they exist, and they demand that we do as well; as we've seen, James insists their own values and needs are closely bound to their worship. In any case, it's clear James would refuse allegiance to any paltry or mean deity—even were it the only supernatural reality on offer.

James is happy with a universe in which a number of gods may exist, among which some may repel us and others call to us as like to like. But he argues strongly that religious believers have always done this: supernatural origin alone was never enough to lend authority to a vision; one still had to decide whether it was good or evil spirit, god or devil. The same was true of miracles: we know whose side to be on in the New Testament, but the gospels show a serious debate about whose power is shown in such acts.

When he was first setting out the need to use a criterion of value rather than origin, he makes a nice statement of this point:

> This criterion the stoutest insisters on supernatural origin have also been forced to use in the end. . . . In the history of Christian mysticism the problem how to discriminate between such messages and experiences as were really divine miracles, and such others as the demon in his malice was able to counterfeit, thus making the religious person twofold more the child of hell he was before,

---

139. Ibid., 301–3.

> has always been a difficult one to solve, needing all the sagacity and experience of the best directors of conscience. In the end it has to come to our empiricist criterion: By their fruits ye shall know them, not by their roots.[140]

In that passage he's arguing for his early distinction between the existential and spiritual judgments. But it serves as well for my point here. James is clearly correct on the problem of discrimination and how well religious traditions themselves have been aware of it. And, to my mind, he gets the better of the dogmatists on its implication for the religious life. As origin in a bad diet isn't enough to discredit mystical visions, so a supernatural power behind them isn't enough to validate them.

It's characteristic, too, of William James that he doesn't necessarily require that the god or gods which stand for his ideals be the most powerful, which probably would separate him from most traditional believers. But James didn't find power as such admirable. As I noted above, if at the bitter end we find only one god who weighs our trivial debits and credits and consigns most of us to the fire for eternity, James, no doubt feeling human values were being trampled on, would probably challenge the right of such a being to the title of "God," thinking—to borrow a defiant gesture from Milton—it is better to suffer in hell for defending human values than be rewarded in heaven for their defeat.

Now that we've exposed the machinery of James's spiritual judgment and explored the heart within it, let's take a closer look at how the actual judgment works out.

The immediate luminousness of religious experience is something that is implicitly argued for by James simply by quoting accounts of such experiences. That religious experiences are felt to be tremendously important and come with an irresistible power becomes clear from the cases he cites:

> As a matter of psychological fact, mystical states of a well pronounced and emphatic sort *are* usually authoritative over those who have them. . . . The mystic is, in short, *invulnerable*, and must be left, whether we relish it or not, in undisturbed enjoyment of his creed.[141]

---

140. Ibid., 26.
141. Ibid., 381–82.

To those of us outside such experiences, the only way to show they are immediately luminous is by the accounts given by persons who have had them. This verdict is given to us by the entire book: it is so much a part of the work that James hardly needs to give it explicitly. As I've been saying, these accounts are both a presentation of what James considers the true religious life and a broadening of the possibilities of human life as such. This probably stands as the major effort and achievement of *The Varieties*.

I'll put off until the next section the narrower issue of philosophical reasonableness: how religious claims harmonize with our philosophical and scientific beliefs about the world. It's the broader sense of philosophical reasonableness, how religious aspirations harmonize with our other spiritual and moral ideals, that's at work when James weighs the value of saintliness, as well as the moral helpfulness of the saintly character.

James organizes his discussion around a list of saintly qualities which, again, seem more a rough way to sketch a kind of character than a strict attempt to define an essence. As always, James's lists tend to mutate as he goes along and, as always, his lists and their changes have their own story to tell.

When he begins his discussion of saintliness, he lists four "practical consequences" of the "fundamental inner conditions" of the saintly life: asceticism, strength of soul, purity, and charity.[142] Interestingly, he sketches charity first, and even more interestingly, he sketches it through the violent history of Richard Weaver I discussed above and rounds off the sketch with a catalog of self-immolating saints who "cleaned the sores and ulcers of their patients with their respective tongues."[143] Then, when he moves on, instead of returning to this original list, he offers a new list of what the faith-state brings: equanimity, resignation, fortitude, and patience.[144] After concluding the "Saintliness" lectures with a celebration of the virtue of poverty, he begins "The Value of Saintliness" lectures with yet another list: devout love of God, purity, charity, and asceticism. Again, the strenuous life of the ascetic provides the final climax and gains the highest praise.

As a contrast, if I were to present a list of saintly qualities, I would use a more traditional list. I would begin with the cardinal virtues: prudence, justice, temperance, fortitude; I would end with the theological virtues: faith, hope, and charity. Setting this beside James's lists, I think we can see two things. First, there seems to be a balance in the traditional list between

142. Ibid., 251.
143. Ibid., 261.
144. Ibid.

inner qualities and public acts, where prudence, or good judgment, and justice, for example, are clearly virtues that function in a social context, and James really lists nothing like them. Faith has a two-sided quality, implying both believing (or trusting) and what is believed (or trusted); devotion, or devout love of God, which seems the closest thing to faith James offers, is very much on our side of the balance, and, anyway, is only on one of his lists. The second thing we can see is that my list climaxes not in the ascetic life but in faith, hope, and charity, or love, the greatest of these being love. It's hard to read the "Saintliness" lectures and not conclude James is trying to get charity out of the way so he can address more stirring virtues. (It's also hard not to marvel at the extremes of his discussion.) Charity has a greater place in "The Value of Saintliness" lectures where one might say, of the four named qualities, only two abide, charity and asceticism; but the greatest of these is asceticism.

In fact, if James has hard words for religious experience itself, beyond the flaws and distortions of institutions, they will be found in his discussions of devotion and purity. As we've seen, and as would be obvious to anyone reading The Varieties, James wants to locate all the failures and the evils of religion in its institutions, with their corporate corruption, their politics, their dogmatism and lust for power. I suppose almost anyone who sets out to defend religion from the horrors done in its name will be tempted to make this claim, and there's certainly much truth in it. But James is a concrete and honest thinker, and when he's looking closely at devotion and purity, he can't wash clean the jealous force and the aggressive rage for order they bring to the religious life.

Thus, despite all his bias toward the individual, he admits it's the experience of devotion itself that gives birth to fanaticism: "the deity's enemies must be put to shame."[145] James sums up the fanaticism of the devout with an indictment that includes some of his heroes, and this passage is worth hearing in our time, when wholesale accusations and equally wholesale defenses of religion are commonly heard and commonly clash in futility:

> The saintly temper is a moral temper, and a moral temper has often to be cruel. It is a partisan temper, and that is cruel. Between his own and Jehovah's enemies a David knows no difference; a Catherine of Sienna, panting to stop the warfare among Christians which was the scandal of her epoch, can think of no better method of union among them than a crusade to massacre the

145. Ibid., 311.

Turks; Luther finds no word of protest or regret over the atrocious tortures with which the Anabaptist leaders were put to death; and a Cromwell praises the Lord for delivering his enemies into his hands for "execution." Politics come in in all such cases; but piety finds the partnership not quite unnatural. So, when "free thinkers" tell us that religion and fanaticism are twins, we cannot make an unqualified denial of the charge.[146]

I heard, while working on this writing, two different speakers mount a defense of religion by arguing that most of the supposedly religious atrocities of our day were really disguised forms of national and political conflicts. So I think James's judicious reflection is worth repeating: "Politics come in in all such cases; but piety finds the partnership not quite unnatural." No, not quite.

It's equally impressive to me that James was willing to trace the source of some of the most obvious and obviously hateful abuses of corporate religion to the virtue of purity:

> ... the love of God must not be mixed with any other love.... sensitiveness and narrowness, when they occur together ... require above all things a simplified world to dwell in. Variety and confusion are too much for their powers of adaptation.[147]

And so the aggressive piety of the church militant reaches purity "by forcibly stamping disorder and divergence out ... with its prisons, dragonnades and inquisition methods."[148]

And yet, despite this honesty and clarity, there seems to be a sense in *The Varieties* that such things may have seen their day. Certainly, my younger self had the strong impression that James was impatient with devotion and purity because of their more passive extremes. The stories of Margaret Mary Alacoque, so blissed out on divine love she was hopeless at the simplest task, and Louis of Gonzaga, so protective of his virginity he couldn't even look at female relatives, provide some of the comic relief of *The Varieties*, but those are the stories that conclude James's discussions of devotion and purity; and my sense is most readers would get the impression that those virtues are flawed primarily because they produce useless, cloistered lives, not because they lead to massacres and pogroms.

---

146. Ibid., 312.
147. Ibid., 317.
148. Ibid.

On Religious Life: William James and I

It's the withdrawal from the world, the selfish pursuit of personal holiness, that bothers James the most, and he notes this as one way our sense of reasonable ideals differs from earlier eras:

> Smitten as we are with the vision of social righteousness, a God indifferent to everything but adulation, and full of partiality for his individual favorites, lacks an essential element of largeness; and even the best professional sainthood of former centuries, pent in as it is to such a conception, seems to us curiously shallow and unedifying.[149]

This is another passage I happily nodded along with a half-century ago. I thought a vision of social righteousness could only bring the blessings of peace, racial justice, equality, caring, sharing, and all the other good things we write hymns about. It never occurred to me that the fanaticism and the aggressiveness James noted in the past would not die out but would flourish again in my lifetime. It never occurred to me that some visions of social righteousness could involve the worst abuses of jealous devotion and aggressive purity. Ethnic cleansing, racial hatred, and male disgust for women may all have other sources, but, as James might say, religious purity finds its partnership with them in our time not quite unnatural.

In the end, however, it's the saintly qualities of asceticism and charity that James rests his positive judgment of religion on, and here I find I'm in closer agreement with both James and my younger self.

When addressing these qualities, James remains alive to the abusive or dangerous extremes they might give rise to. However, the extremes of asceticism or selfless love raise different problems than those of devotion and purity. I want to rearrange James's order and deal with charity last because, when James is puzzling over its extremes, I think he gives the clearest statement of how he sees saintliness transforming the world; also, it seems to me, though not to James, that charity has a direction and power that the ascetic life in itself lacks.

But, for James, it really is the ascetic life, the life of self-denial, harsh discipline, endurance, and poverty, that is the highest we can aspire to. It's the jewel in the crown of the religious life: it's there we find its glory writ large in legends of suffering and sacrifice, but it shows us all what we can be. If you want a vivid proclamation of James's vision of the Good Life, read the concluding sections of both the "Saintliness" and "The Value of Saintliness" lectures. Even when presenting its extremes, in gruesome detail, James

---

149. Ibid., 315.

seems more fascinated than revolted. He pities Henry Suso, who devises one ghastly way to torture himself after another, yet he respects both the drive to self-discipline and the sheer endurance of pain more than he could ever respect the romantic swoonings of Margaret Mary Alacoque.

The strenuous life, for James, is the true life, yet he fears it may be passing from the modern world:

> A strange moral transformation has within the past century swept over our Western World. We no longer think that we are called on to face physical pain with equanimity. It is not expected of a man that he should endure it or inflict much of it, and to listen to the recital of cases of it makes our flesh creep morally as well as physically.[150]

But this is a life that cannot satisfy:

> Passive happiness is slack and insipid, and soon grows mawkish and intolerable. Some austerity and wintry negativity, some roughness, danger, stringency, and effort, some "no! no!" must be mixed in, to produce the sense of an existence with character and texture and power.[151]

In modern life, James still finds what he's looking for in adventure, athletics, and military life. He remarks on "the beauty" of war in how it fits the needs of ordinary human nature for effort, endurance, heroism, freedom from care, and scorn of death.[152] The warrior fascinates him as much as the self-torturing monk, though the warrior calls to him more deeply. Yet it's the cruelty and carnage of war that finally throws him back to the saints:

> But when we gravely ask ourselves whether this wholesale organization of irrationality and crime be our only bulwark against effeminacy, we stand aghast at the thought, and think more kindly of ascetic religion.... I have often thought that in the old monkish poverty-worship, in spite of the pedantry which infested it, there might be something like that moral equivalent of war which we are seeking. May not voluntarily accepted poverty be "the strenuous life," without the need of crushing weaker people?[153]

---

150. Ibid., 273.
151. Ibid., 274.
152. Ibid., 331.
153. Ibid., 332–33.

On Religious Life: William James and I

Poverty becomes for James a kind of governing virtue. He writes of the "mysteries" it contains: the satisfaction of self-surrender, the clear-eyed view of the world's harshness, the revelation that a life of being brings us more than a life of having.[154] Most intriguingly, he says in poverty we find "the mystery of democracy, or sentiment of the equality before God of all his creatures."[155] A more traditional writer would have tied self-surrender to faith and equality before God to both faith and charity. But, for James, these are mysteries that are opened to us by a life of poverty. This clearly shows how central this notion was for him. It shows as well how he strongly felt virtue needed an anchor in a particular way of living.

But it wasn't just the physical and moral strength of voluntary poverty that attracted James, and it wasn't just the fear of pain that he saw weakening us. James strikingly ends his presentation of saintliness and its value with a polemic against wealth and worldly success:

> ... the desire to gain wealth and the fear to lose it are our chief breeders of cowardice and propagators of corruption. There are thousands of conjunctures in which a wealth-bound man must be a slave, whilst a man for whom poverty has no terrors becomes a freeman. Think of the strength which personal indifference to poverty would give us if we were devoted to unpopular causes. We need no longer hold our tongues or fear to vote the revolutionary or reformatory ticket. Our stocks might fall, our hopes of promotion vanish, our salaries stop, our club doors close in our faces; yet, while we lived, we would imperturbably bear witness to the spirit, and our example would help to set free our generation. The cause would need its funds, but we its servants would be potent in proportion as we personally were contented with our poverty.[156]

Before moving on to charity, I have two observations about James's treatment of asceticism.

First, the idea of a moral equivalent of war was quite popular when I was studying James. I remember the Peace Corps, with its combination of voluntary service and peaceful activity, being discussed in terms of such an equivalent, which seemed fair enough. But the real war in Vietnam was also much on my mind, and most of the people going off to it weren't seeking the strenuous life: they were going to war because they'd been drafted.

---

154. Ibid., 296.
155. Ibid.
156. Ibid., 334.

The war itself wasn't started as a strenuous adventure: it came about by a series of foreign policy decisions. That is, there are both legal and political dimensions to war beyond whatever psychological or spiritual appeal it might have. Thus, something like the Peace Corps, regarded as diplomacy seriously pursued by peaceful means, might count as a moral equivalent to war. But if we see that war has a political dimension, it's nonsense to think voluntary poverty or monastic discipline could replace it. This really is a place where James's tendency to see psychological similarities betrays him. Also, James was horrified by the carnage of war; that's why he wanted a moral equivalent. But I fear that today too many of us see the carnage as a mark of serious engagement with the world's problems. We engage in diplomacy for years and get nowhere, and we say we've been fools; we drop bombs for years *and get nowhere,* and we say we're determined. We in America have nurtured a faith in violence, nationally and personally, that would have stunned William James. The destruction, for us, is the very point of war.

My second observation also has to do with James seeing the monk and the warrior as exemplifying the same virtue. But here, granting the real similarity of devotion, sacrifice, endurance, and the other qualities a life of ascetic discipline contains, we can see, in the wildly different contexts monk and warrior flourish in and the wildly different consequences they bring to the world around them, how dangerously empty a merely formal virtue like asceticism is. I was at a literary conference many years ago where the panelists began discussing the lack of moral fiber in young people, their indifference to things beyond themselves, as old people love to do. This happened to be when the conflict in Northern Ireland seemed particularly hopeless, and there was an Irish poet on the panel. She said she could introduce all the panelists to young people in her country who were models of devotion and sacrifice, who threw away their lives in service of a greater cause, who endured whatever suffering they met; then she said: and what they do is plant bombs in mailboxes and bridal shops and restaurants that kill and maim men, women, and children, and it's horrible.

I think, reading *The Varieties,* a problem like this never stands out because James himself gives the strenuous life content by his obvious goodness and compassion. He also leads us to the ascetic life through his discussion of charity, a virtue that only exists in turning from self *to others in love.* Its radiance implicitly fills the discussion of asceticism with a definite content and direction, and it's really those virtues together that constitute the summit of saintliness for James.

Because of its essential content, the extreme pursuit of charity offers a different problem than the other saintly virtues. It's the monastic temptation James fears the most, a person being warped and distracted from worldly affairs, being of no use to anyone. But charitable or loving saints aren't in danger of fleeing the world for the pursuit of their own holiness: their problem is their going forth with too much trust and tenderness. This may be dangerous or even fatal to them. (One line I've never forgotten from *The Varieties* is this: "There are saints whose beard you may, if you ever care to, pull with impunity."[157]) More importantly, in being tender or forgiving towards all, the saint may forgive someone or something that the world needs to fight and to rid itself of:

> ...reasonable arguments, challenges to magnanimity, and appeals to sympathy or justice, are folly when we are dealing with human crocodiles and boa-constrictors. The saint may simply give the universe into the hands of the enemy by his trustfulness.... The whole history of constitutional government is a commentary on the excellence of resisting evil, and when one cheek is smitten, of smiting back and not turning the other also.[158]

George Orwell was notoriously impatient with idealists and, in a famous essay on Gandhi, makes this very point, wondering how non-violent resistance would fare against Hitler's Germany. In James's terms, the extremes of charity ignore the important human ideal of fighting evil, not forgiving hateful and hideous deeds, not allowing brazen oppression to go unresisted. James declares to his listeners the natural agreement with this he assumes they have:

> ...you believe in fighting fire with fire, in shooting down usurpers, locking up thieves, and freezing out vagabonds and swindlers.[159]

Yes, they do. And then he points out how much they would hate a world in which no one ever rose above such harshness. (This, by the way, is an excellent example of how a preacher in a sermon gets a congregation to confront itself and to realize the limitations of its easy prejudices.) Without the living examples of the saints, the world would be infinitely worse:

157. Ibid., 336.
158. Ibid., 323.
159. Ibid., 324.

> The tender grace, not of a day that is dead, but of a day yet to be born somehow with the golden rule grown natural, would be cut from the perspective of our imagination.[160]

Here James speaks both for the visionary force of the saints and for the practical, transforming force of the saints, and this is his most powerful statement of their moral helpfulness, their being in themselves a creative social force. He writes another fine concluding hymn in praise of charity and offers a powerful answer to the charge that loving, nonviolent saints leave the world to the monsters:

> Treating those whom they met, in spite of the past, in spite of all appearances, as worthy, they have stimulated them to *be* worthy, miraculously transformed them by their radiant example and by the challenge of their expectation. . . . Force destroys enemies; and the best that can be said of prudence is that it keeps what we already have in safety. But non-resistance, when successful, turns enemies into friends; and charity regenerates its objects. . . . This practical proof that worldly wisdom may be safely transcended is the saint's magic gift to mankind.[161]

James has one more point to make for the saints and, in a fascinating decision, he develops it by allowing Nietzsche's voice to pour scorn on the saintly impulses and exalt the conquerors, the "beaked and taloned graspers of the world."[162] This comes at the very end of "The Value of Saintliness" lectures, and James seals his judgment by contrasting the worlds of the ruthless and the saintly, noting the conserving force the saint brings to life, in addition to the creative force:

> The saint is therefore abstractly a higher type of man than the "strong man," because he is adapted to the highest society conceivable, whether that society ever be concretely possible or not. The strong man would immediately tend by his presence to make that society deteriorate. It would become inferior in everything save in a certain kind of bellicose excitement, dear to men as they now are.[163]

---

160. Ibid.
161. Ibid., 324–26.
162. Ibid., 336.
163. Ibid., 339.

As I've lived with *The Varieties* over the years, I've come to appreciate the long discussion of saintliness and its value more and more and to see it as central to James's achievement, both in *The Varieties* and in his philosophy as a whole. (My younger self was most fascinated, I recall, by conversion and mysticism.) As I've made clear, I see both the nature and the problems of religion differently than James does. Some of my disagreements come from his basic approach and some from the world that has changed around me. James can hardly be said to be judging religion itself, as he claimed he was, and I'm less and less sure, much less sure than I was, that such a judgment would make any sense. Judging religion is like judging the wind: there's enough to celebrate and enough to condemn for any judgment to be plausible.

But his presentation of the spiritual heroism he admired, strenuous lives of expanding compassion, lives that create a better world by living as though it's already here, is so clear and passionate that it becomes an undeniably splendid thing, whatever it's called. That James found what he admired in some of what's called religion is probably less important than his gathering up and proclaiming it as a human ideal.

This brings me to my last point. It struck me strongly, as I again studied James's praise of charity and asceticism and his assertion of their creative force, that saintliness becomes an experience in itself. That is, what's transforming the people and the world around the saint isn't mystical vision or the force of the subconscious: it's the encounter with the saint. Saintliness almost becomes a self-propagating life. It's possible to wonder why James needs to speak of a subconscious realm or why he needs any gods at all.

But he certainly thought he did, and it's to those matters I'll turn in my concluding section.

6. Search for a Spiritual Landscape

I recall a sense I had, when I first approached the concluding sections of *The Varieties*, of groping in front of me for something I couldn't quite grasp. It was like almost remembering a word or a name, like the rising and falling frustration of not quite sneezing, like trying to make out a face in a dream. Part of this came from James himself putting off again and again any weighing of the truth of religion, as well as qualifying and hedging anything definite he did say. Mostly, though, my frustrated sense of incompletion came from my own wanting to be told something neither James nor anyone else was ever going to be able to tell me: the absolute and final truth about all things, as well as how exactly we might acquire such certain knowledge. I would say, looking back, I was more obsessed with issues of knowledge and truth than I realized.

Reading over, all these years later, my first version of this concluding section, it struck me as the slipperiest of my chapters, the most wandering and indecisive. I could see both how hard I was trying to please my dissertation advisor, Dr. Rowe, and why he would remark that anyone who wrote *on* James seemed eventually to write *like* James. I think now that my own obsessions were preventing me from seeing clearly what James was trying to do and what he would settle for.

At the beginning of the *Pragmatism* lectures, he quotes favorably one of Chesterton's clever paradoxes: that the most practical and important thing about people is their view of the universe, their philosophy.[164] It's the sort of remark young philosophy students love to hear, something they can repeat to their parents and skeptical friends. But, James goes on, that important philosophy "is not a technical matter; it is our more or less dumb sense of what life honestly and deeply means."[165] Here was the difference between my young self and William James: I would instinctively understand philosophy in a much more technical sense.

Thus, thinking purely as an academic, I could pretend to myself that settling what we know about the universe must come first, before any discussion of how to live in it. But James always saw life as more than knowledge and a human being as more than a knower; he never lost the sense he had of life carrying us along, making it necessary for us to proceed provisionally. For James, we *may* know, but we *must* live, so we have to get on with it with whatever we have so far.

I think I was disappointed that James couldn't give me a list of things I could believe in unquestioningly, even though I really did know he was the last philosopher I should expect that from. What I thought should have been the climax of *The Varieties*, the discussion of the truth of religion in the strictest sense, its claims about the universe, I now think of as necessarily anticlimactic for James himself.

I see his concluding lecture now as expanding a picture of the universe out of the saintly lives he proclaimed as valuable, filling in a kind of background that would be adequate for, or worthy of, the heroic figures

---

164. Ibid., 487.
165. Ibid.

he had already defined. He was looking not so much for a defense of the truth claims of religion as for some way of conceiving a universe that would sustain the qualities he admired, a spiritual landscape just real enough to make strenuous and expansive lives worth living.

When he was singing the praises of asceticism, he made one of his standard claims to be speaking only what we commonly believe:

> In these remarks, I am leaning only upon mankind's common instinct for reality, which in point of fact has always held the world to be essentially a theatre of heroism.[166]

Setting aside the truth or falsehood of that sweeping claim, the passage still gives us an insight into what James is setting out to do: he will construct that theatre for his saints; he will give us a picture of the universe in which those lives make sense. He will build that picture out of all he can find in experience that's promising and suggestive. He will make it as realistic as he can, but it's first and foremost a theatre of heroism, called forth more by how we are than how the universe might be in itself.

So, in this version of my concluding section, I want first to discuss why James rejects the arguments for the truth of religious claims that might be offered by mysticism and philosophy. I'll look then at what James thinks he can offer as a hypothesis, based simply on the power and suggestiveness of religious experience, and explore the picture of the universe he comes up with. Finally, I'll end by gathering up some of his remarks that offer an alternative way of seeing all of experience as a living, animated drama; it's a line of thought drifting along here and there in the corners of the lectures but takes shape near the conclusion as a fascinating suggestion and adds some vivid color to the picture James is painting.

But first let's look at what James found to say about truth taken in its strictest sense. It's hard not to see him as simply getting this issue out of the way, a necessary but distasteful task. One of the things my younger self had a hard time seeing was his impatience in these sections, especially with the logical arguments of philosophy; I also failed to appreciate how overwhelmingly important, to James, were the rich experiences, the high ideals, and the transforming moral power he had already praised religion for bringing. I kept accusing him of "mixing" these questions up with the question of truth and blurring the issues; James would say he was reminding us of the important questions in order to clarify the issues.

---

166. Ibid., 330.

James says, after discussing the value of saintliness, that he will turn to mysticism to evaluate its claim to ground religion in truth. But he spends most of the "Mysticism" lectures quoting more of the witnesses that fill his study, and he laments the "extreme brevity and insufficiency" of his presentation. Here's what he finally offers as a characterization of mystical consciousness:

> It is on the whole pantheistic and optimistic, or at least the opposite of pessimistic. It is anti-naturalistic, and harmonizes best with twice-bornness and so-called other-worldly states of mind.[167]

Then he frames the question about truth this way: Does the mystical consciousness itself "furnish any *warrant for the truth* of the twice-bornness and supernaturality and pantheism which it favors?"[168]

This strikes me as both a surprising way to put the question of truth and one fairly typical of James. It could be accused either of hopeless vagueness or unnecessary complication: why not just ask whether or not mystical experience implies the existence of a supernatural power?

But I think putting it so directly would reduce it to another form of the cosmological argument. If mysticism is to offer anything special, it must be along the lines of its special characteristics. James is asking something like: *Must* mysticism force us to see the falseness or at least the limitation of something like a commonsense view of the universe?

James gives a many-sided answer and, of course, it's the suggestiveness of mysticism that he will use to push us toward not so much settling as allowing that question. But as it's stated—Does it furnish any warrant for the truth of its claims?—the answer is a fairly clear no. I want to look first at the reasons behind this no and then at the more promising things he sees in mysticism.

His strongest complaint against mysticism, as it relates to the issue of truth, is that the testimony of mystical writers is not as unanimous as it is often claimed to be.[169] As I noted in section four, James primarily stressed the variety of creedal commitments entered into by mystics; he also saw all religious experiences as varying by temperament. If we add to this the presence of traditional imagery in the experience itself, the unanimity claim loses even more of its force.

---

167. Ibid., 381.
168. Ibid.
169. Ibid., 383.

But James makes the point stronger: even if the testimony of the world's mystics were unanimous, it would prove nothing, one way or the other, about its truth, especially when a large part of the world is on the other side:

> At bottom, however, this would only be an appeal to numbers, like the appeal of rationalism the other way; and the appeal to numbers has no logical force.[170]

Thus, mystical experiences can't serve to establish any theoretical claims because there is only a weak unanimity where even a strong would not suffice.

This is the most telling argument James raises against the mystics. But he continues by presenting a further problem which shows how much more important to him are questions of conflicting ideals, authority, and power. He points out there is "another half" of mysticism:

> In delusional insanity, paranoia, as they sometimes call it, we may have a *diabolical* mysticism, a sort of religious mysticism turned upside down. The same sense of ineffable importance in the smallest events, the same texts and words coming with new meanings, the same voices and visions and leadings and missions, the same controlling by extraneous powers; only this time the emotion is pessimistic: instead of consolations we have desolations; the meanings are dreadful; and the powers are enemies to life.[171]

It's a powerful, vivid passage and one sure to infuriate anyone impatient with James's tendency to declare two experiences or phenomena "essentially the same" that he himself, following other lines of argument, would claim differed in every important respect. He continues by tracing the origin of both mysticisms to the "great subliminal or transmarginal region" where "'seraph and saint' abide" together, another claim which, as we've seen, brings its own problems. Then he concludes this way:

> To come from thence is no infallible credential. What comes must be sifted and tested, and run the gauntlet with the total context of experience, just like what comes from the outer world of sense.[172]

---

170. Ibid., 383–84.
171. Ibid., 384.
172. Ibid.

William James and the Gods (Revisited)

But "no infallible credential" for what? James had turned to mysticism, and will proceed to philosophy, with the specific intention of discussing truth, after his own discussion of value. He did, in fact, speak to that issue. But here he reverts to the question of value: Which gods are we to follow? What James is supposed to be discussing is: Are there supernatural powers and realities to begin with? It's irrelevant to say that the subconscious is the home of both benevolent and malevolent powers: the question of truth still remains (or rather: James has already settled it by his first point). Also, the mystics themselves, as James clearly stated elsewhere, were quite aware of this. It would be wholly consistent for a believer to claim that both good and evil spirits could enter human experience, as well as to grant that our values must play a large part in testing them: neither admission implies an answer, and certainly not a negative answer, to the question of whether or not mystical experiences establish the existence of anything supernatural. That James concludes his rejection of mysticism's truth claims with this point shows how the issues of value and authority helplessly outweigh for him the issue of truth.

Much the same thing happens in his discussion of philosophy.

The first point he makes is that intellectual constructions and arguments by themselves could not support the religious life, that they are mere "by-products" of experience:

> I doubt if dispassionate intellectual contemplation of the universe, apart from inner unhappiness and need of deliverance on the one hand and mystical emotion on the other, would ever have resulted in religious philosophies such as we now possess.... These speculations must, it seems to me, be classed as over-beliefs, buildings-out performed by the intellect into directions of which feeling originally supplied the hint.[173]

As I argued in section four, the relation between religious experience and religious philosophies is more complex than James wants to admit. But the important point to notice here is that he again shifts the issue. It's one thing to claim that logical arguments, if sound, can provide the foundation and spur of the religious life or make zealous converts to that life; it's quite another to claim that logical arguments, if sound, can provide some support for the religious life by increasing its intellectual respectability. James has no patience with the first claim; the entire effort of *The Varieties* is set against it. But refuting the first claim doesn't refute the second, and

---

173. Ibid., 388.

it's the second claim that James should be discussing. He again reveals how much of a hold the issues of value and creative power have on him and how limited he thinks logic to be in the religious life. Most of his discussion of philosophy seems to avoid the very issue that caused him to begin it.

However, at one point he presents an argument that I remember smiling over. It seems to be yet another variant of his scornful dismissal of rationalism, but I think it amounts to more than that. I don't take it to be merely psychological, as it might be accused of being, and it does seem to offer a valid, if weak, reason for rejecting truth-claims based on philosophical argument.

James wants to avoid something he would scarcely have the patience for, a point-by-point confrontation with the arguments for the existence of God. Thus, he wants an argument which will defeat them *en masse*. He comes up with this: supposing the point of logical arguments to be the attempt to establish universally the truth of certain propositions, to convince, if not everyone, at least most reasonably fair and rational people, then it is an adequate test of those arguments to ask if they *have* been so convincing:

> It will suffice if I show that as a matter of history it fails to prove its pretension to be "objectively" convincing. In fact, philosophy does so fail. It does not banish differences; it founds schools and sects just as feeling does.... The arguments for God's existence have stood for hundreds of years with the waves of unbelieving criticism breaking against them, never totally discrediting them in the ears of the faithful, but on the whole slowly and surely washing out the mortar from between their joints.[174]

In this passage, James is arguing once again for the general superiority of feeling over reason in the passionate affairs of life; and it would be tempting to say that he has once again lost sight of the real issue. But, in so arguing, he is attacking the claim that the arguments of philosophy are, or can be, objectively convincing, and I think this really does speak to the point at issue. It's one thing to claim that you can avoid the subjectivity of belief by an objective method of argument: presumably, the value of a logical argument is that it can do this, that it can ideally satisfy everyone. But, James argues, it would be extremely odd to claim you had an argument which could satisfy everyone but which in fact satisfied fewer and fewer people. This is a more than psychological claim; that is, James is not merely saying that the arguments don't *feel* convincing to him. Also, this isn't an

---

174. Ibid., 392.

appeal to *popular* feeling. He isn't appealing to any feelings of conviction at all, but to the history of those arguments in philosophical debate. This seems a fair enough judgment and seems adequate for James's purposes.

What this means for the spiritual judgment is that a crucial part of it (and one James admittedly tends to ignore) remains unsatisfied: neither mystical vision nor philosophical argument allow us to take the philosophical reasonableness of religion as in any way established. Further, this would clearly be the point at which any defense of religion, any claims for its value, would be weakest. What James said about the arguments for the existence of God could be said about all religious claims that had any implications at all about the nature of life and the universe: the history of philosophical debate, while not discrediting them, has steadily eroded them. And there the judgment might rest, with the value of religion resting on the power of religious experience and the transformative force of saintly lives. (In fact, it would probably be easy to gather a number of passages from James's work where he seems to do just that.)

But James doesn't let it rest there. He really does want to say something about the wider universe, about the place of faith in the human adventure of knowledge, about some way the visions of faith might find a foothold beyond human feeling. More importantly, he thinks he's justified in doing this by the very strangeness and unusual power of mystical experiences.

That is, mysticism doesn't offer evidence for the truth of religion, but it does offer its own mysteries as a challenge to our understanding. It has merely suggestive, not logical, force; but the suggestive force, in James's eyes, is powerful. Mystical experiences force us to acknowledge the possibility that the universe is wider than the "non-mystical or rationalistic consciousness" is willing to allow:

> They break down the authority of the non-mystical or rationalistic consciousness, based upon the understanding and the sense alone. They show it to be only one kind of consciousness. They open out the possibility of other orders of truth, in which, so far as anything in us vitally responds to them, we may freely continue to have faith.[175]

Again, mystical experiences do not establish the truth of religion; James is as clear on this as any atheist could be. But they do open out possibilities for understanding the truth of things differently, real possibilities

---

175. Ibid., 381.

for believer and nonbeliever alike. This might be a fine line to walk, but it's a line James was comfortable strolling down:

> Mystical states indeed wield no authority due simply to their being mystical states. But the higher ones among them point in directions to which the religious sentiments even of non-mystical men incline. They tell of the supremacy of the ideal, of vastness, of union, of safety, and of rest. They offer us *hypotheses*, hypotheses which we may voluntarily ignore, but which as thinkers we cannot possibly upset. The supernaturalism and optimism to which they would persuade us may, interpreted in one way or another, be after all the truest of insights into the meaning of this life.[176]

James is reaching for something which can be at least (and at most) possibly true. Inevitably, of course, we meet again the problem of exactly what the hypotheses suggested by mystical experiences are. We saw earlier that James thought the immediate experience might be captured by several conceptual systems; we saw as well that he had too simple a view of creeds and their relation to religious life. I think James probably thought the hypotheses he cautiously elaborated captured a fairly large element of most traditional faiths (or at least the element he thought was authentic), but I don't think he found that comparative issue very interesting in itself. He was interested in what religious experience suggested about the life we all lived.

So, with the suggestiveness of mystical experience, let's pick up two more elements with which James constructs his hypotheses.

First, there's the subconscious. As I said, in section two, the subconscious is the primary psychological concept used by James in *The Varieties*, and he used it early on to illuminate, and perhaps normalize, the experience of conversion. But he sees it, more broadly, as a basic element in all religious life:

> When, in addition to these phenomena of inspiration, we take religious mysticism into the account, when we recall the striking and sudden unifications of a discordant self which we saw in conversion, and when we review the extravagant obsessions of tenderness, purity, and self-severity met with in saintliness, we cannot, I think, avoid the conclusion that in religion we have a department

---

176. Ibid., 386.

William James and the Gods (Revisited)

of human nature with unusually close relations to the transmarginal or subliminal region.[177]

But just as it could, in a sense, normalize religious experience, it can also make strange ordinary experience. It offers a mystery of its own, a bridge out of the normal, sunlit world, a kind of accessible arena in which James can plausibly picture divine forces at work.

Second, James has definite and fairly typical modern ideas of how a deity might act in the world. Just as, on moral grounds, he rejected a feudal concept of the divine character, so he also rejects, with most of the scientific community, the concept of a deity who can physically act on the forces of nature:

> Notwithstanding the recency of the opposite belief, everyone now knows that droughts and storms follow from physical antecedents, and that moral appeals cannot avert them.[178]

(I fear it would now be news to too many Americans that "everyone" knew droughts and storms could not be averted by moral appeals. In any case, as it stands, that statement can no longer be made without qualification. The rise of American fundamentalist Christianity, and its entrance into public life, has brought with it an ignorant assault on education in general and science in particular. It has managed to cripple the knowledge of and respect for science in America, something James would probably find incomprehensible. I think there's a sense in which praying to escape danger is helplessly inevitable for believers, even for those with the weakest of faith. James himself considers "Help! help!" among the most primal religious appeals. But what marks American fundamentalists is their scorn for science, often tied to political causes, and the rigid moral causality they project on natural disasters. It's one thing to pray for help in a storm; it's another, uglier, thing to blame all disaster, natural storm or human violence, on God's displeasure with women's rights or the acceptance of homosexuality. Here both the moral and the cosmological regression come together.)

But how does James see the action of God? On his own terms, there has to be a pragmatic difference, new facts, a difference here and now that God makes in the world. Let's continue with the above passage:

> But petitional prayer is only one department of prayer; and if we take the word in the wider sense as meaning every kind of inward

177. Ibid., 433.
178. Ibid., 415.

communion or conversation with the power recognized as divine, we can easily see that scientific criticism leaves it untouched.[179]

James thus arrives at a vision of divine action that every liberal protestant, perhaps every liberal believer of any sort, in the modern world has probably produced some variant of:

> Through prayer, religion insists, things which cannot be realized in any other manner come about: energy which but for prayer would be bound is by prayer set free and operates in some part, be it objective or subjective, of the world of facts.[180]

What should be stressed here is that James is talking about more than feelings or attitudes: it's the *energy* unleashed in prayer, the powerful unification and concentration of the person that he analyzed in the conversion experience, the force that issues in a new life, that brings a real difference to the world.

Thus, mystical experience, the subconscious, and prayer provide James a suggestive set of phenomena from which he can envision a spiritual landscape greater and richer than we might normally imagine.

James's final articulation of what goes on in religious experience, the view he will test for philosophical reasonableness, is very much tailored to the subconscious and the conversion experience. When he finally comes to discuss the question of truth in his concluding lecture, he begins by describing "a certain uniform deliverance in which religions all appear to meet," and we are very much back with the divided self and the process of its unification:

> It consists of two parts:–
>
> 1. An uneasiness; and
>
> 2. Its solution.
>
> 1. The uneasiness, reduced to its simplest terms, is a sense that there is *something wrong about us* as we naturally stand.
>
> 2. The solution is a sense that *we are saved from the wrongness* by making proper connection with the higher powers.[181]

Those so divided feel themselves torn between their own wrongness and something better which is at least calling to them. When they achieve

---

179. Ibid., 415–16.
180. Ibid., 417.
181. Ibid., 454.

their unification, they identify their real selves with that something better, something higher. James in effect gives his final, minimalist formulation of the immediate judgment on religious experience in secular terms which come as close to mystical union as possible:

> *He becomes conscious that this higher part is coterminous and continuous with a MORE of the same quality, which is operative in the universe outside of him, and which he can keep in working touch with, and in a fashion get on board of and save himself when all his lower being has gone to pieces in the wreck.*[182]

There are a couple of obvious problems this passage raises which have to be addressed so we can clarify what exactly James is offering.

First of all, how seriously are we to take the claim that "all" religions meet in this uniform deliverance? We have seen James go back and forth on this issue, depending upon what he wants to emphasize, but it was particularly when he was discussing mysticism's truth claims that he denied the uniformity of mystical experience. So can he legitimately allow himself to claim it here?

I think it's clear he wants to emphasize a uniformity here that he wouldn't claim elsewhere, but I don't think it's of great consequence. In the first place, his remarks on mysticism were meant to show no *proof* could begin from the fact that mystics unanimously testified to an identical experience because, in fact, they didn't. Here, he has no intention of offering a proof but only a suggestion he considers plausible. He doesn't need to qualify his characterization because he doesn't intend to put it to any rigorous use. In the second place, as we'll see, his suggested hypotheses are based less on any common nucleus than on the nature of the subconscious and the experience of something that seems beyond the self.

This brings us to the second problem. I remarked earlier, when I was comparing James's various descriptions of religion's essence, that this characterization he gives in his concluding lecture seemed too obviously tailored to fit his notion of the subconscious. He doesn't always use such loaded terms, and it's a real question whether what he says here can adequately characterize even his own examples. The healthy-minded seem to offer a different, less tortured, process of unification, and some of the tortured, like John Bunyan, never seem to find unification. This seems another

---

182. Ibid.

time when what James wants to get out of religious life forces him to use a narrower and narrower slice of it.

Again, I'm not sure how great a problem this is. James is not really setting out at this point to capture an essence of religion. He began with a pretty definite idea of what that was. But here he's looking for something in religion that he can use as a kind of launching pad for speculation, something that can reasonably force us to look beyond the ordinary.

To sum up, then: James's characterization of religion wasn't offered either as a guarantee of any truth claims or as a serious way of capturing religion's essence. He wanted a way to describe religious experience (without trivializing it) in fairly nonreligious terms. By tying it so closely to conversion and the subconscious, he has what he considers to be a clear way of locating divine action in the world. In a conversion experience, James can point to what he calls "a place of conflux where the forces of two universes meet."[183] Finding a place like that is what's important to him at this stage of the argument. From here, he formulates two hypotheses: one, a small, cautious step; the other, a great leap.

As we saw at the start, James thought the subconscious qualified as "a well-accredited psychological entity."[184] And since it harmonizes so well with his final characterization of the religious life, his first hypothesis comes easily:

> Let me then propose, as an hypothesis, that whatever it may be on its *farther* side, the "more" with which in religious experience we find ourselves connected is on its hither side the subconscious continuation of our conscious life.[185]

Leaving open the question of what, if anything, is involved on the farther side, James thinks the subconscious, with its scientific credentials, really does allow him to say that "the sense of union with the powers beyond us is a sense of something, not merely apparently, but literally true."[186] Even if it has not been shown that divine intervention is taking place, mystics are not wrong that new stores of energy are opened for them; they may be wrong about what the higher powers are, but they're not wrong to think

---

183. Ibid., 455.
184. Ibid., 457.
185. Ibid., 457–58.
186. Ibid., 458.

they're in connection with these powers. James states this as strongly as he can:

> We have in *the fact that the conscious person is continuous with a wider self through which saving experiences come*, a positive content of religious experience which, it seems to me, *is literally and objectively true as far as it goes*.[187]

So far James considers himself on solid ground. But how wide is the "wider self"? What is the "farther side" of the "more"? More pointedly, there's a serious problem with James's easy talk of a "farther side" of consciousness. We'll have to return to this. For now, let's look at his second hypothesis, one sketching out the nature of those "farther limits of this extension of our personality."[188]

Here, apparently, he is much less sure of his ground, since he willingly stamps *this* hypothesis an "over-belief".[189] But we are now being given, in these final pages of *The Varieties*, James's most concise presentation of his vision of the world, that which he said was the one great fact about a person. He remarked in the postscript that a later work might state his position more completely.[190] Presumably, he had in mind something like *A Pluralistic Universe*. But at the close of *The Varieties*, with hundreds of bloody, haunted, and terror-filled documents still fresh in our minds, we hear James speaking in what must count as his own element. Here we sense the despair and the urgency, the truly religious tone of James's thought.

The violent, personality-shattering experiences of the world's mystics, combined with James's belief that the gods act in the world through their contact with us, yield the following picture of the universe:

> The whole drift of my education goes to persuade me that the world of our present consciousness is only one out of many worlds of consciousness that exist and that those other worlds must contain experiences which have a meaning for our life also.[191]

Indeed, those worlds are our true home, as we are, in this world, the bearers of the ideals we find in them:

---

187. Ibid., 460.
188. Ibid.
189. Ibid.
190. Ibid., 464.
191. Ibid., 463.

> The further limits of our being plunge, it seems to me, into an altogether other dimension of existence from the sensible and merely "understandable" world.... So far as our ideal impulses originate in this region ..., we belong to it in a more intimate sense than that in which we belong to the visible world, for we belong in the most intimate sense wherever our ideals belong. Yet the unseen region in question is not merely ideal, for it produces effects in this world. When we commune with it, work is actually done upon our finite personality, for we are turned into new men, and consequences in the way of conduct follow in the natural world upon our regenerative change.[192]

I got the sense that these worlds of consciousness could be taken as the homes of the gods or, perhaps, the gods themselves. James seems to have in mind a kind of freely floating consciousness which is still supposed to be a person-like deity. For the most part, our own world remains separate from these greater powers, "yet the two become continuous at certain points and higher energies filter in."[193]

It is important to realize that this second hypothesis is not offered by James as an explanatory hypothesis invoked to cover the otherwise unexplainable phenomenon of religious experience. It is a hypothesis about the ultimate nature of reality that is based on religious experience and James's analysis of it. Religious experience, if one can say James explains it, is explained by the subconscious. It's the unexplored, open-ended nature of that strange entity that gives James's picture of the world the possibility of being true. And, again, it's only the possibility of truth that James is claiming for this second hypothesis.

James calls his position crass or piecemeal supernaturalism: supernaturalism, to distinguish it, for obvious reasons, from naturalism; piecemeal, to distinguish it from "refined" supernaturalism, which would allow the existence of ideal realms but admit of no connections between them and our own poor natural existence.[194] (I had to smile again at James's delight in opposing crass to refined realities, even in worlds beyond us.)

There are basically two things involved in piecemeal supernaturalism: the connections between our world and the world (or worlds) beyond us and the nature of God (or the gods).

---

192. Ibid., 460–61.
193. Ibid., 463.
194. Ibid., 464–65.

William James and the Gods (Revisited)

We have seen how seriously James takes prayer; it seems to him both a well-attested reality and an example of a clear difference that faith brings to the world:

> If asked just where the differences in fact which are due to God's existence come in, I should have to say that in general I have no hypothesis to offer beyond what the phenomenon of "prayerful communion," especially when certain kinds of incursion from the subconscious region take part in it, immediately suggests.[195]

More interesting, though, is that, as James understands faith and its witnesses, something more is needed; the practical effects must "embrace a wider sphere than this."[196] Mystical experience and prayerful communion can't in themselves exhaust the whole sphere of divine action; in that case, we might simply be giving pious names to facts wholly bound to this world. The difference made by anything divine must amount to more than that:

> God's existence is the guarantee of an ideal order that shall be permanently preserved. This world may indeed, as science assures us, some day burn up or freeze; but if it is part of his order, the old ideals are sure to be brought elsewhere to fruition, so that where God is, tragedy is only provisional and partial, and shipwreck and dissolution are not the absolutely final things.[197]

Now for the second, equally intriguing aspect of piecemeal supernaturalism, where James states outright what one might have suspected all along. Though both philosophers and mystics have instinctively felt drawn to a supreme and single reality, James see no compelling reason either in logic or experience to move so firmly in that direction:

> ... the practical needs and experiences of religion seem to me sufficiently met by the belief that beyond each man and in a fashion continuous with him there exists a larger power which is friendly to him and to his ideals. All that the facts require is that the power should be both other and larger than our conscious selves. Anything larger will do, if only it be large enough to trust for the next step. It need not be infinite, it need not be solitary.[198]

---

195. Ibid., 466–69.
196. Ibid., 462.
197. Ibid.
198. Ibid., 468.

James allows that the larger thing we trust might only be a larger self, with the universe being only a collection of such selves.

But his whole sense of what religion is and who the gods might be is tied very closely, not only to humanity, but to *struggling* humanity. I quoted, in section four, a passage from early in the concluding lecture, when I wanted to illustrate that James's defense of religious diversity was based on his sense of what diverse lives needed. I want to highlight this passage again here. First note the sense of individual struggle, of being thrown into life:

> No two of us have identical difficulties.... Each, from his peculiar angle of observation, takes in a certain sphere of fact and trouble, which each must deal with in a unique manner. One of us must soften himself, another must harden himself; one must yield a point, another must stand firm,—in order the better to defend the position assigned him.[199]

Softening or hardening, all the choices are seen by James in the language of battle: "to defend the position assigned." He follows that reflection immediately by alluding to a diverse quartet selected from his choir of witnesses. But note here that the human diversity not only demands but seems to serve a divine diversity. Not only humanity but the gods themselves would suffer from religious uniformity. The polytheism is bursting to come out:

> If an Emerson were forced to be a Wesley, or a Moody forced to be a Whitman, the total human consciousness of the divine would suffer. The divine can mean no single quality, it must mean a group of qualities, by being champions of which in alternation, different men may all find worthy missions. Each attitude being a syllable in human nature's total message, it takes the whole of us to spell the meaning out completely. So a "god of battles" must be allowed to be the god for one kind of person, a god of peace and heaven and home, the god for another.[200]

If we could, then, stay close to the testimony of religious experience itself and remain sensitive to human diversity, if we could at least glimpse the richness of divine possibilities, then, James concludes, "would a sort of polytheism return upon us."[201] He's quick to say, in his postscript, that he's not going to defend this polytheism, though I wondered what more he

---

199. Ibid., 436–37.
200. Ibid., 437.
201. Ibid., 468.

could do to defend it than he had already, by writing *The Varieties*. But he's equally quick to declare, as he does for so many of his positions, that this polytheism, distasteful as it might be to intellectual elites, "has always been the real religion of common people, and is so still today."[202]

So much for my exposition of the universe and our life within it according to William James, speaking on behalf of the people of the earth.

In the first version of this study, I closed this section by discussing several possible criticisms of the position James takes in his conclusion. Most of my discussion was, I might say, academically inevitable, trotting out current writers in the philosophy of religion, revisiting the issues of the nature of consciousness, the efficacy of prayer, and the scope of scientific explanation, and leaving James pretty much where he was, where most great philosophers are: not invulnerable to objections, but not defenseless either. It was all understandably fussy and overdone. The most serious problem I had was with the subconscious as James developed it in his conclusion. The most interesting defense I constructed for James came from some charming remarks he made on animistic and anthropomorphic thought. This passage struck me as both more interesting and more promising than the subconscious, as well as putting on splendid display the heart of what James was as a thinker. So I'll close this version of this work by saying a little about the subconscious and a little more about the liveliness of the world.

I noted earlier in this section that I would return to the issue of the "farther" side of consciousness, so let's look again at James's first hypothesis:

> Let me then propose, as an hypothesis, that whatever it may be on its *farther* side, the "more" with which in religious experience we feel ourselves connected is on its *hither* side the subconscious continuation of our conscious life.[203]

What bothered me about this immediately was James's offhand reference to a "farther" side which seemed, suddenly, a bit farther off than it had earlier. When James first discussed the subconscious and illuminated the conversion experience, it seemed to me the subconscious simply *was* the farther side of consciousness, the hither side being what was central to our awareness at any given time. But here James speaks as if the subconscious were part of the *hither* side of consciousness with its own farther reaches.

---

202. Ibid.
203. Ibid., 457–58.

This struck me as a completely unjustified assumption. Once the subconscious is introduced, we seem to have all we need to explain the sense of otherness, of outside control, of the "more" encountered in religious experience. How much of a farther side does the "more" need? Admittedly, James's further claims are given only as possibilities; but the point is they seem unnecessary and unjustified additions that the experiences in question really don't require.

In section two, I distinguished between an empirical and a nonempirical conception of the subconscious. Not only does James seem unaware of this ambiguity, but nothing he says about the subconscious makes the stronger conception more plausible, while some of the speculations he bases on the subconscious require that stronger conception for their own plausibility. This is what happens in his conclusion. He leaves open the question of what the farther side of the MORE is really like, pleading ignorance; but because of his stronger conception of the subconscious, he feels certain that there is a farther side, one that is, moreover, so rich in possibilities that he feels entirely justified in speaking of other realms of consciousness which produce effects in our own. Again, this last hypothesis is labeled pure speculation. But it's the earlier hypothesis which allows the speculation, and it does that by making implicit use of a conception we've been given no reason to accept.

As *The Varieties* grew, so grew the subconscious. Early on, James seemed to be working with the tamer conception. At the end, the sketchiness of his conception allowed him to sail out on a speculative sea, with less of a scientific entity under him than he thought.

This seriously weakens his attempt to establish the philosophical reasonableness of any broad claims based on religious experience and weakens further his positive spiritual judgment on religion. James offered the subconscious and the interlocking realms of consciousness as the crowning discussion and the official conclusion of his study. I think, obviously, the real crown and conclusion lie elsewhere, as does his heart.

Earlier in his concluding lecture, however, he paused to reflect on a sort of global scientific dismissal of religion as such, the "survival theory" of religion, which sees it as an atavistic survival we should have outgrown long ago. It's here he presents a view of experience that leaves the subconscious behind and offers, in my view, a more fitting conclusion to his journey.

I noted above that I was more narrowly obsessed by knowledge and truth than James was, that James always saw life as more than knowledge and a human being as more than a knower. This, despite decades of superficial criticism by people who only seem to have glanced at his writings, does not mean he was unconcerned with truth and rationality. No serious student of James can doubt his respect for knowledge and human reasoning. But for James this was one need among many; *knowing* was only one of humanity's many powers, and not necessarily the most important. (I suspect the power of fighting for our lives, in every sense, might hold that place.) I think James really is close here to the common human outlook: we face reality as more than knowers.

(Charles Peirce famously disliked James's will-to-believe argument, but his objection to it revealed their differences with stunning clarity: Peirce thought no individual's destiny could be momentous enough to justify taking a leap of faith in the absence of knowledge. This would be an impossible position for William James.)

But James would insist on something more, something that affects the very nature of human knowing: those who face a thing as more than knowers *see more of that thing* than if they had only assumed the attitude of knowledge seekers. The aspects of a thing revealed in this way should not be ignored for being more impressionistic than measurable.

James argues for this in *The Varieties*, and it's near the heart of his defense of religion:

> The pivot round which the religious life, as we have traced it, revolves, is the interest of the individual in his private personal destiny. Religion, in short, is a monumental chapter in the history of human egotism. The gods believed in—whether by crude savages or by men disciplined intellectually—agree with each other in recognizing personal calls. Religious thought is carried on in terms of personality, this being, in the world of religion, the one fundamental fact. Today, quite as much as at any previous age, the religious individual tells you that the divine meets him on the basis of his personal concerns.[204]

If our mode of thought has changed at all, says James, we have become more interested in those aspects of things that allow us to get a handle on them. Our ideals of knowledge are less centered on personal interests and anxieties, we scorn anthropomorphic thinking, we're impatient with religious visions and purposes:

---

204. Ibid., 439–40.

Pure anachronism! Says the survival theory;—anachronism for which deanthropomorphization of the imagination is the remedy required. The less we mix the private with the cosmic, the more we dwell in universal and impersonal terms, the truer heirs of Science we become.[205]

Against this, James puts his objection in a nutshell:

> ... so long as we deal with the cosmic and the general, we deal only with the symbols of reality, but as soon *as we deal with private and personal phenomena as such, we deal with realities in the completest sense of the term.*[206]

We shouldn't let the impersonal ideals of knowledge blind us to the richness of ordinary experience and to how natural it is to respond to things in this way:

> ... it is still in these richer animistic and dramatic aspects that religion delights to dwell. It is the terror and beauty of phenomena, the "promise" of the dawn and the rainbow, the "voice" of the thunder, the "gentleness" of the summer rain, the "sublimity" of the stars, and not the physical laws which these things follow, by which the religious mind still continues to be most impressed; and just as of yore, the devout man tells you that in the solitude of his room or of the fields he still feels the divine presence, that inflowings of help come in reply to his prayers, and that sacrifices to this unseen reality fill him with security and peace.[207]

James was in San Francisco during the earthquake of 1906, and he wrote of the experience very much along these lines. A friend of his from California had joked that he hoped he might encounter one:

> "By Jove," I said to myself, "here's B.'s old earthquake after all!" And then, as it went *crescendo*, "And a jolly good one it is, too!" I said...
>
> The emotion consisted wholly of glee and admiration; glee at the vividness which such an abstract idea or verbal term as "earthquake" could put on when translated into sensible reality and verified concretely; and admiration at the way in which the frail little wooden house could hold itself together in spite of such a shaking. I felt no trace whatever of fear; it was pure delight and welcome.

205. Ibid., 446.
206. Ibid.
207. Ibid.

William James and the Gods (Revisited)

> "*Go* it, " I almost cried aloud, "and go it *stronger!*"
> ... I personified the earthquake as a permanent individual entity.... It came, moreover, directly to *me*. It stole in behind my back, and once inside the room had me all to itself, and could manifest itself convincingly. Animus and intent were never more present in any human action, nor did any human activity ever more definitely point back to a living agent as its source and origin.[208]

I remember lying on my bed in college during a mild earthquake. While my bed slid around the room and the pictures flapped against the walls, I kept wondering how the guys in the dorm were making it all happen. In such dramatic cases, the sense of a personality behind the act is almost irresistible. But it can happen on a more day-to-day level as well. I had forgotten my coat one day while bicycling to the university. It was late fall and I was terribly chilled, especially after I parked my bike and trudged across a draughty, shadowy courtyard. To make things worse, there was a coal strike on and I was worried about winter heating. My bones were rattling from the present and projected cold. But it was one of those days which are dreadfully chilly when cloudy and instantly warm when the sun reappears, and as I crossed the mall I was suddenly standing in the sunshine, completely warm. I stopped, raised my arm, and said, "Thank you."

I suppose I was talking to the sun, although the gesture was so spontaneous as to be almost without a definite object. I will admit as readily as anyone that the sun could not have *intended* to *give* me some warmth because I was in a bad way. Yet there it was. I offered my thanks, as one small creature to a greater one. I guess I'm disposed to think that's not such a negligible moment.

The claim James wants to make is that moments like these are just as, if not more, important in our total relationship to reality than any scientific knowledge we have about those same objects. The claim is about more than us: we're seeing a thing with all it has, at its fullest, a reality in the completest sense. To throw away nature's lively face for a scientific diagram is to throw reality out the window:

> A bill of fare with one real raisin on it instead of the word "raisin," with one real egg instead of the word "egg," might be an inadequate meal, but it would at least be a commencement of reality. The contention of the survival theory that we ought to stick to

---

208. Ibid., 1215–16.

non-personal elements exclusively seems like saying that we ought to be satisfied forever with reading the naked bill of fare.[209]

I want to try to distinguish what James is saying here from something I thought was a natural and a common move in the theist-atheist game played in the philosophy of religion during the twentieth century, which I touched on briefly in section three: that religious belief wasn't so much a set of claims about the world, which might be true or false, as an alternate way of seeing the world, in which questions of truth and falsehood could only arise internally, but not about the way of seeing itself. (This proposal was a little like Collingwood's Absolute Presuppositions, perhaps more like Thomas Kuhn's paradigms, but neither comparison is exact.) I usually associated this move with the little line drawing made famous by Wittgenstein: tilted one way it looks like a duck, tilted another way it looks like a rabbit. The drawing doesn't change; the point of view changes; both are valid. So: the atheist sees the sun rise at dawn or, with more sophistication, sees the effect of the rotation of the earth as it orbits the star which, along with many other random factors, makes life possible until it won't any more; the theist sees the dawn of a new day, God's gift of light and life and the splendor of creation, rising to shine in praise of the creator, as Christ rose from the dead with the glory of a new life, etc., etc.

But William James proposes that we see *the promise of the dawn*, and *both* theist and atheist should be able to see that. (Also, importantly, *both* might *fail* to see it.) James is pointing out a richness in life itself. He doesn't see it as one interpretation of a neutral reality that might be named in different ways: he sees it as the truest description of that reality. Duck and rabbit interpret the same line drawing; what James is getting at is the difference between a line drawing and a live animal.

This becomes part of his defense of religion because he thinks religious traditions are more alive and alert to such aspects of reality, just as religious life has a way of foregrounding the strenuous life. But, as always with James, he's talking about life and experience as such, and his later philosophy moves very much in this direction.

He can put this very strongly, and I thought he verged on claiming that all things needed some sort of personal awareness to exist at all:

> That unsharable feeling which each one of us has of the pinch of his individual destiny as he privately feels it rolling out on fortune's

---

209. Ibid., 447–48.

wheel may be disparaged for its egotism, may be sneered at as unscientific but it is the one thing that fills up the measure of our concrete actuality, and any would-be existent that should lack such a feeling, or its analogue, would be a piece of reality only half made up.[210]

This would certainly mesh well with James's polytheism. We could almost envision ourselves in a world where every tree had a soul. But what I liked most about this line of thought was that it spared me the problems I was having with James's use of the subconscious, not to mention the farther worlds lying beyond it. What had impressed James about the subconscious was the apparent encounter with higher powers. But that's just what he asks us to see in the promise of the dawn and the power of the earthquake. I also liked that, with this view, he doesn't divide the world into what science can explain and what it can't. Instead of isolating divine intervention to one small part of reality, he argues that, given a scientific explanation of *all* phenomena, there is still more to be said about them on the basis of our experience. I thought, if he had highlighted this discussion a bit more, he might have called himself, instead of a crass or piecemeal supernaturalist, a glorified naturalist.

I spent the conclusion of my original version of this study weighing how much or how little James's animistic view of life contributed to the philosophical reasonableness of religion. Oddly, I now think, I concluded it didn't contribute much. I lamented how *The Varieties* fell apart, but celebrated how fascinating and stimulating James's writings remained, how they always, much like the dawn, glowed with promise.

But I had been seeing and presenting James's animism as an alternative to the subconscious and the speculations he based on that. Once again, I think I was missing a deeper connection and a deeper purpose.

I would now say that everything in his concluding remarks, including his polytheism, was meant to expand the world for us, push the limits of experience, deepen and enrich the world both in its depths and on its surface. He wanted to use everything he could to enliven the world, to bring out its possibilities and challenges, temptations and threats, higher allies and lower demons, risks and rewards. He wanted to envision a world worthy of the saints and their struggles. I would now say he was as successful as he thought he needed to be.

---

210. Ibid., 447.

On Religious Life: William James and I

I've loved returning to *The Varieties* over the years. I've tried, in this last formal visitation, to clarify the lines of argument in my early version, but I hope I've also managed to highlight more clearly the broader aspects of James's work. I think it's endured as it has and appealed to so many because it's much more than an attempt to define the nature and evaluate the worth of religion: it's a journey through human experience with William James. No one should miss that trip.

Part Four

Ave Atque Vale

1

As I get nearer to becoming one of the people of the past myself, it's been interesting to look back on the thinkers, scholars, and artists who were part of my life and work and see which of them remained vividly present to me and which faded away. A few years ago, I actually made up a semiformal list: I was invited to contribute an essay to a collection on the film director Sam Peckinpah and how his work has endured for those who first wrote on him forty years ago. Peckinpah himself had certainly been one of my constants; but I reflected a bit on this issue of which artists last a lifetime, and here's what I wrote:

> Looking back on the artists and thinkers I've followed in my life, I'm surprised by some that have remained and some that haven't. I'm surprised I don't read Dickens that much, and I'm surprised I reread Spinoza's *Ethics* so often. I watch fewer John Huston movies than I thought I would. I'm very surprised that I couldn't stay interested in Godard.
>
> On the other hand, there are thinkers and artists, old and new, I return to so regularly that it's odd to speak of returning. Certainly I never have to rediscover them. William James, Melville, Kipling, the poet David Jones, Hemingway, and Philip Roth have accompanied me through the years. So have John Ford, Wilder, and Welles.[1]

---

1. Strug, "Human Striving, Human Strife," 139.

This wasn't meant as an exhaustive list. If it had been, Samuel Johnson and Karl Barth, to mention only two, would have had to be on it. Also, by the nature of the collection, my list was heavily weighted toward narrative artists. It's all the more striking, then, that James made the top of the list, and it says something about the place he held in my life.

I would like, in this final part, to try to give a sense of what a touchstone James has been for me by gathering up some of the times and some of the ways he has surfaced in my life over the years.

2

I was teaching confirmation class one day, and we were doing the doctrine of creation. I always tried to make my students aware of the unsystematic and unscientific variety of biblical reflections on creation: we went through the first two chapters of Genesis in detail, so they'd know there were two creation stories that differed significantly in sequence and detail; I'd point out that the *Christian* story of creation only came in the first chapter of John's Gospel; I'd show them the lovely passage about Wisdom in Proverbs 8, which tells yet another version of how the world came to be. I'd also go through the Big Bang theory of the universe's beginning and try to show how stupid it was to fight about it. I'd do the same with evolution.

Our classes were usually small, and I think there were about five students there the day I'm thinking of. Sitting across from me was a boisterous, athletic girl named Mickey, who usually nodded her way sleepily through class and tended to drive me crazy. I was doing my usual rant on the ignorance of "Creationism" and "Intelligent Design" and I had them look at the verse where God forms Adam from the earth.

"See, basically," I said, "This isn't that different from what Darwin was getting at—that we're all made of the same stuff. We come from the earth, the mud. I mean, we're swamp slime . . ."

A couple of students laughed.

"This is why it's so dumb for Christians to keep fighting about evolution. It's one of the dumbest fights—"

Mickey sat straight up and slapped her hands on the table. Her eyes were wide and bright. In fact, I rarely saw her so awake. She was smiling wickedly.

"*You* believe in evolution?"

"Yeah. Of course. I mean, scientists still fight about the details, but, yeah, in general, the argument's over."

"But you *can't*," she said. "You're a *pastor*."

I think I said something like: "Yeah, but I'm not an idiot. So I do. You're just going to have to cope with that."

I offer this story as evidence of how closely American Christianity came to be linked with scientific ignorance. Mickey kept smiling during that class: I think she was tallying up how many of her Assembly of God friends she could provoke with the story of my embrace of Darwin. I also suspect it may have been the first time she thought I might be a sensible person.

But this episode comes to mind here because I remember thinking after class: "If I just bit my tongue and allowed my students to think I agreed with all the ignorance being pushed by Christian conservatives, I'd be too ashamed to ever read a book by William James again."

It would be too much to say James was responsible for my interest in science, but the example of his vast curiosity was certainly part of the reason I cultivated it. More than that, however, it was his welcoming mind, his openness to ideas, and his wariness of human pride, how it can refuse to see the truth of things, especially the messy truths of the earth, that gave me an image to live up to and something I didn't want to betray.

3

When I retired, I decided I'd carried around my old course notes and academic papers long enough for one lifetime. If I hadn't needed my comparative charts on the synoptic gospels or my graduate seminar paper on Leibniz's *New Essays Concerning Human Understanding* during the preceding thirty years, I was unlikely to need them during the next thirty, should there be that many. Most of them are now enriching some central Minnesota landfill.

Some I kept, including one manila folder labeled "W. James papers." I remembered compiling it, some time after I left the academic community, but was mildly surprised by what I found in it. There were both handwritten and typed copies of complete papers, as well as twenty or so pages of handwritten notes and quotations from James's writings, all of them held together by rusty paper clips. There was an offprint of my published article on the subconscious mind in *The Varieties* and the text of my seminary lecture on James, with a nice thank-you note from Dean Terry Fretheim. But there were also two other papers, one of which I'd entirely forgotten.

Interestingly enough, it's a paper on "James and Evolution," complete with a dazzling set of notes ranging over all James's writings. It also has written comments and a thank-you note at the end, instead of a grade. It's possible I produced it for an independent study with a seminary professor who was interested in the topic. It strikes me as a fairly typical, plodding academic survey, but I like the confident, sweeping judgment it begins with:

> Shortly after the death of William James, Josiah Royce claimed a place for him beside Edwards and Emerson as the greatest of American philosophers. It is a judgment that has never been called into question, and while Anglo-American academic fashion has preferred more mathematically modeled philosophies the stature of James as a figure of a kind of golden age has not lessened.
>
> This is no accident. The philosophical movement of which James was a part (with Wright, Peirce, Santayana, Royce, and Dewey) stands as the one modern philosophical movement to give a relatively coherent response to the tensions of 19th century thought—scientific, mathematical, religious and artistic. Just as the philosophers of the 17th century recast the whole of philosophy in response to the development of physics, so the pragmatists recast the whole of philosophy in response to the investigations of their day—and primarily to the theory of evolution.[2]

I recognize with fondness both the magisterial tone and the gallery of beloved thinkers I had hoped to spend a lifetime studying and writing about.

I did remember the other paper fairly well, since I had attempted to publish it. It had a title I thought was both clever and a little edgy: "Once Is Not Enough: James on Mysticism." (The journal I submitted it to was outraged that I would allude to a current soft-porn novel.) It was the second paper I wrote based on my dissertation, and it dealt with the place of mysticism within religious traditions, but it had one aspect I imagined would mark my future writings: I set off James's position by writers from outside the philosophical community. My title was not simply an allusion to Jacqueline Susann's *Once Is Not Enough* but referred as well to a passage in a fairly obscure novel on spiritualism by William Dean Howells, *The Undiscovered Country*, where a Shaker points out that to encounter the miraculous once was quite enough to build a life on. I also quoted Thomas

---

2. Strug, "James and Evolution," 1.

Merton on the contemplative life and the Rule of St. Benedict on the necessity of monastic discipline.

I had, for a time, thought I might continue writing scholarly papers, academic position or not. But, being out of the game, I eventually had to admit they would be little more than an exercise in vanity. Looking back now, I marvel that I ever considered doing anything so tedious.

I had much more fun with the kind of writing I ended up doing in my sermons. They too would be marked by references beyond the normal: movies, novels, poetry, and philosophy. I felt my academic background gave me something I could bring to sermons that would be a little unusual. I thought sometimes that my situation as a writer and thinker might be a little like Arthur Sullivan's when he wrote his comic operas with Gilbert. Sullivan's classic training and high aspiration as a composer brought something different to the popular art of the theater and produced something unique. You could even say the theater gave his music a freedom it didn't otherwise have.

I hoped I could do something similar in my work, and that I might find a similar freedom. But I know I had fun doing it.

4

While I was serving as a pastor, I kept the part of me that was neither pastor nor philosopher alive and well by writing a series of novels, none of which were published but all of which I enjoyed constructing. The one I had the most fun with was called *If You Lived Here, You'd Be Home Already*. (I saw a sign like this as I was driving through a small town near Fargo, North Dakota. I think they meant it to sound inviting.) This was about 1988 and I was getting tired of people praising "small town values," especially since that slogan was often only a disguise for racism and other bigotries. Besides, I liked city life, so I thought I'd concoct a comedy about an urban person driven home to the town he'd escaped as a way of portraying the downside of rural life. I made my urban person a church organist and choir director, coming home after losing his job to live with his father, a lawyer who scorned both religion and art. On Christmas, the son, James, named not for William but for an organist of my acquaintance, was looking for a present as a kind of bridge between them. I had him choose William James:

> He had saved his father's present for this morning. Over the years, his father had sent him a check each Christmas and he had sent

a card. But dwelling in the same house seemed to call for some extra effort. Since a tree would have been going much farther into the season than his father would consider, James had kept the gift upstairs and he handed it to his father after breakfast.

He had bought him the Library of America edition of the writings of William James, hoping it might serve as a common ground between them. For his father, it would be a volume by an old Yankee, a philosopher of the democratic spirit; for James, it would be a Yankee with an open mind, as far as the less quantifiable aspects of existence were concerned.

McGrath, to James' surprise, seemed genuinely pleased.[3]

My choosing James's writings as a bridge between adversaries was certainly no accident. A great part of James's presence in my life was as a bridge of understanding. Especially as a church worker in a small town, I was in constant friction with the kind of church leaders who made my confirmation students think pastors shouldn't believe in evolution. Having absorbed James so deeply, I was given a limiting force for my scorn and my anger. More positively, I had an unshakable awareness that truth was many-sided, that there were many strains of piety, and that there were aspects of human nature that were probably beyond my grasp. James helped inoculate me against dogmatism. This didn't stop my scorn or my anger in all cases—it didn't stop James's either—but it softened them.

5

Not that I couldn't be stirred up in other ways.

Just as important, for the intellectual and political climate I served in, was the pragmatic view that many of our arguments and confusions are rooted in a failure to look beyond the words we're using. The admonition to look for the difference being made was a lamp of truth in a time when the language of religion and of value was being hijacked by some of the uglier forces in our society. If it was important to be aware that two differently stated theories might amount to the same thing, it was equally important to realize identical words could hide a world of difference. I grew wary of church programs described as "biblical" or "faith-based," and suspicious of laws described as "patriotic," intended to preserve "freedom" or "human rights." I wouldn't even open mailings from anything called "Heritage" or

---

3. Strug, "If You Lived Here, You'd Be Home Already," 375–76.

"Family Institute." All the words were lovely, but the realities were something else.

6

Above my desk, over the years, I liked to paste pictures of people I admired (Virginia Woolf, Samuel Beckett, others) and quotations I thought might inspire me (from Machiavelli, Pauline Kael, others). Here's one from James that was among the first I put up:

> ... to be a real philosopher all that is necessary is to *hate* some one else's type of thinking ...

I'm not sure where I found this remark. I would guess it was from one of his letters. I think I liked it because I realized fairly early in my life that my liveliest writings—philosophical, fictional, or theological—were generated by things that infuriated me. But it shows an aspect of James I appreciated as much as his generosity: his sense of struggle, his indomitable spirit, his pugnacity, usually exercised on behalf of something overlooked or someone left out.

One of the remarks about James I came across very early in my studies that I've never forgotten was from a fascinating writer named John Jay Chapman: "all the dogs were underdogs to James." I thought that was a perfect characterization and comes to me often as a summons to a way I think I ought to be.

7

During my last years of service as a pastor, the United States was fighting its unnecessary and apparently endless wars in Afghanistan and Iraq. Looking back, after I retired, one of the things that bothered me most about my service was how little and how timidly I had spoken about those wars. I was disgusted with the military cheerleading of conservative Christians, but I myself only spoke about the wars when I felt forced to.

One of the times I did feel forced to was on Memorial Day weekend, during the war years, especially as the Iraq war was going sour. I thought it might be interesting to collect my sermons from those days and use them to reflect on the tension of pacifism and patriotism in my life. So I put together a little book called *The Other Cheek: Gospel, Empire, and Memory* in *One Christian's Journey*. I thought it might say something about that time and about what was happening in the country.

As I was looking up epigraphs for the book's sections, I remembered that James was a strong critic of the Spanish-American War and the country's slide into imperialism. I thought a quote by James from that time would serve as a measure of that slide. I had just been reading Barbara Tuchman's portrait of the Western world before World War One, *The Proud Tower*, and I was struck by the title of her section on the United States: "End of a Dream." While I was lamenting the decay of democracy by our imperial policies in the twenty-first century, people like James and Mark Twain were proclaiming the end of one American dream, the dream of a free people as a force for freedom, before the twentieth century began. The passage I used from James was from his "Address on the Philippine Question" to the New England Anti-Imperialist League:

> The country has once for all regurgitated the Declaration of Independence and the Farewell Address, and it won't swallow again immediately what it is so happy to have vomited up. . . . It has deliberately pushed itself into the circle of international hatreds, and joined the common pack of wolves. . . . We are objects of fear to other lands.[4]

When we think of that other famous spokesman for the strenuous life, Theodore Roosevelt, and compare his engagement with the Spanish-American War to James's, we see how utterly different James's conception of that life was. Not surprisingly, he ended the above address in bluntly religious terms:

> Everywhere it is the same struggle under various names,—light against darkness, right against might, love against hate. The Lord of Life is with us, and we cannot permanently fail.[5]

8

On another part of my desk, there's a little reproduction of a drawing by James that I cut out of *The New York Review of Books* years ago. It depicts a man sitting on a chair, his head bowed, his legs spread apart, and his hands on his knees. He looks either stunned by misery or determined to bend no

---

4. James, *Writings 1902–1910*, 1135.
5. Ibid.

further under its weight; either way, he's held by it. Across the top of the drawing is printed: "Here I amid sorrow sit."

I was drawn, finally, by James's melancholy, his strong sense of life's evils, his clear-eyed vision of the tragedies and the pain of life, the exclusions of the cosmos.

Once again, as a church worker, I was grateful for the force of James's presence that kept me close to the truths of the earth. I could never look out on the world and see only the glory and the providence of God. I had little patience with the welcoming light shows of the nearly dead, trips to heaven and angels at the heart of things. I always saw the indifference, the crushing sorrows, the senseless horrors of life.

In the essay on Sam Peckinpah's films that I quoted earlier, I wanted to end by trying to characterize the peculiar quality I saw in his work. I used one of James's protests against the optimists and idealists of his day:

> Is *no* price to be paid in the work of salvation? Is the last word sweet? Is all "yes, yes" in the universe? Doesn't the fact of "no" stand at the very core of life? Doesn't the very "seriousness" that we attribute to life mean that ineluctable noes and losses form a part of it, that there are genuine sacrifices somewhere, and that something permanently drastic and bitter always remains at the bottom of the cup?[6]

I valued that tragic outlook, I liked the pushy questioning, and I loved the exuberance and excitement James gave to even his grimmest thoughts.

9

I've been thinking again of that quotation on my James sweatshirt: "Wisdom is learning what to overlook." I've been thinking, too, of all the ambiguities and happy confusions in James's writings I spent so much time trying to define and clarify.

I wonder now if James wanted deliberately to mix things up, if ambiguity were not his problem but his goal: to soften the edges of human opposition, to urge us toward free and generous understanding.

Anyway, I think if you spend enough time with William James, you forget about his inconsistencies and simply enjoy his company and his wisdom.

---

6. Ibid., 616–617.

On Religious Life: William James and I

So farewell, Professor James. It was a privilege, a pleasure, and a great gift to spend so much time with you while I was here.

Bibliography

James, William. *Writings 1878–1899*, edited by Gerald E. Myers. Library of America. New York: Literary Classics of the United States, Inc., 1992.

———, *Writings 1902–1910*, edited by Bruce Kuklick. Library of America. New York: Literary Classics of the United States, Inc., 1987.

Strug, Cordell. "Human Striving, Human Strife: Sam Peckinpah and the Journey of The Soul." In *Peckinpah Today: New Essays on the Films of Sam Peckinpah*, edited by Michael Bliss, 137–146. Carbondale: Southern Illinois University Press, 2012.

———. "If You Lived Here, You'd Be Home Already." Unpublished manuscript, 1988. Typewritten.

———. "James and Evolution." Unpublished manuscript, 1979. Typewritten.

www.ingramcontent.com/pod-product-compliance
Lightning Source LLC
Chambersburg PA
CBHW071509150426
43191CB00009B/1464